GROW YOUR OWN HAPPINESS

A Buddhist Guide for a Good Life

TSERING PALDRON

TSERING PALDRON

Copyright © 2024 by **Tsering Paldron**

All rights reserved. No part of this publication may be reproduced, distributed or transmitted in any form or by any means, without prior written permission.

Tsering Paldron
www.tseringpaldron.com

Illustrations by Pema Chalmers and Ogyen Namdrol
Cover by Pema Chalmers
Proof reading by Liz Chapman

Book Layout © 2017 BookDesignTemplates.com

Grow your Own Happiness/ Tsering Paldron - 1st ed.
ISBN 978-989-35742-0-1

In reality, the only thing standing in the way of your happiness is you, the only thing holding you back is your mind. It is your mind that equally can help you to see your happiness, to let it colour your day and your life. Happiness is a state of mind.

—GYALWA DRUKPA

TSERING PALDRON

Contents

INTRODUCTION.. 11
CLEARING THE PATH TO HAPPINESS................................. 15
   Accepting responsibility... 17
   Freeing ourselves from guilt 21
   Being gentle with ourselves.. 24
   Developing awareness.. 28
   Familiarising with Meditation 30
   Learning from mistakes 32
   Don't make excuses.. 35
   Avoiding complaints 37
   Change what we can–live with the rest 40
   Feeling grateful... 43
   Keeping a gratitude diary... 46
   Feeling the contentment... 50
   Building a refuge 51
   Cultivating connections 52
   Do what you can, with what you have 55
   Feeling the happiness... 57
   How do we rate our happiness?................................... 59
   The happiness line.. 61

Happiness comes from meaning 62

Practical tips from chapter 1: 64

THE CONDITIONS OF WELL-BEING 67

How to get started 68

Lifestyle 70

Food 71

Health 74

Habits 76

Physical exercise and sleep 78

Creating a harmonious space 79

Ethics 81

Do not kill 83

Do not steal 84

Do not lie 85

Correct sexual behaviour 87

Do not take intoxicants 88

Ethics are a personal matter 89

Practical tips from chapter 2: 92

LIVING FROM THE HEART 93

Interdependent origination 94

Cultivating altruism 97

Cultivating a positive predisposition 100

- Cultivating empathy 103
- Daring to be vulnerable 105
- Compassion vs empathy 107
- Cultivating selfless love 112
- Feeling the joy 115
- Helping others 118
- Finding balance 120
- Practical tips from chapter 3: 124

THE TRUTH OF SUFFERING 125
- The truth of suffering 126
- The causes of suffering 129
- The three types of dukkha 130
- Conflicting emotions 132
- The reality of life 134
- Acceptance, the non-violent approach 139
- Nothing happens by chance 141
- Karma, the causality of actions 144
- Understanding responsibility 147
- Practical tips from chapter 4: 151

BUILDING RESILIENCE 153
- Accept the setback 154
- Nothing lasts forever 157

Have realistic expectations 158

Don't assume bad intentions 159

Stay in the present 161

Nothing is as good or as bad as it seems 163

This too shall pass 165

One day at a time 166

Improve what you can 169

We are not the thoughts 171

Don't hold grudges 173

Avoid escalating aggression 174

Dealing with anger 177

You're not the only one suffering 180

Keep a sense of humour 181

Don't shut yourself in 182

Don't let suffering win 185

Find an outlet 186

How much music can you still play? 187

Don't turn adversity into an obstacle 189

Practical tips from chapter 5: 191

DEALING WITH PAIN 193

Pain is subjective 193

The two arrows 195

- The wise answer 198
- The unlikely answer 199
- Meditation for pain management 203
- Five phases of mindfulness 205
- Wise pain management 212
- Practical tips from chapter 6: 215

SUFFERING AND THE SPIRITUAL PATH 217
- Why do we suffer? 219
- The ego's shell 221
- When the shell breaks 223
- The loss 225
- Filling the void 229
- The greatest loss 231
- Growing old 233
- Empathy and compassion 236
- Contemplation and Prayer 240
- Intention and positive emotions 242
- The one taste 244
- Practical tips from chapter 7 246

GROW YOUR OWN HAPPINESS 247

GUIDED MEDITATIONS 251
- Posture 255

Breathing exercise 258

Refuge and Four Boundless Thoughts 260

Guided meditations 260

Breathing meditation A 260

Breathing meditation B 261

Breathing meditation C 261

Meditation on sensations 262

Meditation on sounds 263

Meditation on space 264

Instant meditation–three conscious breaths 265

Meditation to set an intention at the beginning of the day 266

Meditation to review your day 267

Meditation on impermanence 267

Meditation on gratitude 268

Pain-orientated mindfulness meditation 269

Visualising the Source of Power 271

Tonglen–Giving and Taking 272

The three lights 274

INTRODUCTION

It is very common for Buddhist teachings to begin with the assertion that all beings desire happiness and don't want to suffer but, without fully understanding the causes of happiness, further suffering is often created instead. As depressing as this statement might sound, if we are really honest with ourselves, we can probably recognise that much of our suffering is self-inflicted and completely unnecessary.

This unfortunate state of affairs is even more appalling when we hear that joy, compassion, love and happiness are the natural qualities of our mind and suffering is an altered state that is neither necessary nor inevitable.

According to Buddha's teachings, suffering and happiness both depend on causes and, if we know what to avoid and what to cultivate, not only can we achieve temporary happiness but we can also achieve ultimate peace. In this book I have focused on how to create the relative causes of happiness and on how to deal with adversities, problems, pain and loss in a way that doesn't create any additional and unnecessary suffering. If we learn to accept life as it is and open our hearts to others, we can achieve temporary well-being and thus contribute to creating a better world for all.

There are, of course, Buddhist methods more oriented towards the attainment of Enlightenment, the development of Wisdom or the understanding of Emptiness but you will not find them here. My purpose was much less ambitious. However, even if the ultimate goal of the Buddhist path is a total and irreversible transcendence of suffering, worldly happiness is not excluded and Buddhist methods can also be used for transforming our lives into something more harmonious, imbued with compassion and love, and useful to others. Hopefully, you might find here some useful thoughts, ideas and tips to grow your own happiness.

I was incredibly fortunate to have met with Buddha's teachings at a young age and received countless teachings from many extraordinary teachers of the Tibetan tradition. My deepest gratitude goes to all of them and I only wish I can, somehow one day, repay their kindness. In particular, I want to express my gratitude to Ringu Tulku Rinpoche and Mindroling Jetsun Khandro Rinpoche for their kindness and guidance that have been so precious. I would also like to thank all my spiritual friends for their inspiration, generosity and presence, without which life would be meaningless and this book would not exist.

An earlier version of this text was published in Portuguese–my mother tongue–in 2015. I had never considered publishing it in English until some friends from UK showed interest in it. But it was mostly Carrie Lawson's enthusiasm that motivated me to start the process.

So, the present book has been not only translated but thoroughly revised and updated with the help and support of my dear Liz Chapman. It was she who did all the hard work of proofreading and putting it into form. Without her this book would not have been possible. Last but by no means least, I wish to thank Pema Chalmers for the beautiful art cover that she so generously created–it adds so much to the final result.

There is little in this book that hasn't been explained elsewhere. Countless texts and teachings on *Mind Training* and similar topics have detailed these things and, probably, in a better way. However, considering that even after many good explanations, we sometimes discover a different approach that utterly makes sense to us, maybe this book will provide the key that unlocks your door to happiness. I thus rejoice in any good that may come out it.

TSERING PALDRON

• CHAPTER 1 •

CLEARING THE PATH TO HAPPINESS

Most Tibetan Buddhist teachings on how to transform suffering show us how to deal with crisis, be it illness, material or emotional problems or loss. However, the target audience for these original teachings lived in a very different society, enjoying a very simple, traditional, and natural lifestyle, being part of a community virtually unaware of depression, suicide or mental illness. Today we face those same crises, of course, but must also learn to deal with the stress, anxiety and the fast pace of modern society.

It is increasingly common, these days, for people to live in a state of permanent discomfort and stress that is not caused by any particular situation or crisis. It's simply their most frequent state, a mixture of agitation, fear and anxiety, aggravated by past mistakes or lost opportunities, worries of what the future could bring and resistance to the present. These pressures are not just from internal causes but the burdens placed on us by society.

We hear that happiness is a choice. The realisation that we are the ones who create happiness and suffering by the way we filter and value our experiences is becoming more accepted. But this doesn't mean that all we have to do is make a decision for everything to change instantly. It's not that simple.

Losing bad habits and gaining good ones is perfectly possible, but it requires dedication. It's not like pressing a button or popping a tablet. It's about becoming aware of patterns of behaviour that are largely automatic and that have sometimes been our norm for years. Many of them were passed on to us in childhood by our parents, carers, teachers or friends and then reenacted and reinforced by life experience.

When we have a negative outlook on things, it tends to become a vicious circle. We approach any situation with fear and suspicion, filled with negative anticipation, which, in turn, conditions us to have a negative outlook and behave in a needlessly defensive or aggressive way. Not surprisingly, the outcome is generally not favourable, which in turn reinforces the idea that we were right to be apprehensive. In this way, each new experience reinforces our fears and anxieties, sending us into a destructive spiral from which it is not easy to escape.

Realising that it is our own attitude that determines many of the difficulties and sufferings we encounter and that we have the option of facing them differently is a big step, perhaps the most difficult and essential one. Without it, we will continue to blame others, circumstances or life, never realising our responsibility.

Thanks to this awareness, we begin to observe. Are there situations that recur in our lives? Do we often find ourselves involved in the same kind of conflicts? Do our relationships always end badly? Becoming aware is like waking up. We've tried to find the reasons for our unhappiness, but we've been looking in the wrong place. We've tried to change the world and the people around us, but to no avail. Suddenly we can ask ourselves: Where in my life should I begin a transformation?

Accepting responsibility

It's a radical change of perspective, perhaps a little frightening. We're more used to blaming others, society, the universe or God—as the case may be—and so taking responsibility for our lives can seem uncomfortable. However, if everything depended on other entities, human or divine, we would be totally at the mercy of their goodwill and would only have to try to please and honour them. If we don't believe in providence, we have to hope that there is some justice in the universe and that life's events are not simply random. This prospect is, in fact, truly upsetting.

On the other hand, when we realise that we can change our experience of the world by changing our perspective, we make a fantastic discovery. We realise that, after all, we have the power to change our lives radically and to choose how we want to feel. We don't depend on anyone else to do it. It's empowering and inspiring.

For a period in the early 2000s, I went to Tahiti many times. There was a Buddhist group there that invited me every year to give talks and seminars. At that time there was a plague of an insect called *pissingfly*[1]. The name came from the fact that they suck the sap from trees and then expel a large amount of urine. At the time, there were so many of these insects that if you stood under a tree, you could feel a kind of very fine, sticky rain falling.

On one of my visits, we received Rabjam Rinpoche[2] who came straight from Nepal where, at that time of year, it was still quite cold. The contrast with the hot and humid temperatures of the South Pacific was brutal. On the first morning, we stood under some trees to protect ourselves from the sun and Rinpoche was sweating profusely. He was pleased to notice that there was a small shower of deliciously cool rain and I happily acquainted him with the truth.

At the end of the afternoon, Rinpoche gave a talk in Papeete and, to explain the importance of our perspective in the way we experience things, he recounted what had happened to him in the morning. "While I thought it was rain, I thought it was delightful, but as soon as it was explained to me that it was urine, I got disgusted and immediately went from under the shade."

Though there was no circumstantial change between the moment he was pleased and the moment he was disgusted, his experience had changed radically. This transformation was only due to his change of perspective on the rain. There's nothing unprecedented about this little incident: things like this happen to us all the time, but we usually don't pay attention to them and don't draw any

---

[1] *Homalodisca vitripennis*, from the cicada family.

[2] Shechen Rabjam Rinpoche is an important master of the Nyingma lineage of Tibetan Buddhism. He is the grandson and spiritual heir of Dilgo Khyentsé Rinpoche.

conclusions. However, they can help us realise how our assessment of situations determines how they make us feel.

But we mustn't go to extremes either: of course, not everything in life is our choice. It would be foolish to imagine that illness, natural disasters or economic crises depended on us. Of course, where we are, what we do and who we are is largely the result of successive choices we have made over time. However, the world is such a complex web of interdependencies that not all phenomena could possibly be our responsibility. What is essential to realise is that, even if we don't choose certain events in our lives, we always have the freedom to decide how important they are, how to interpret them and how to respond.

Perhaps we've had difficult experiences in the past (who hasn't?) and feel that we've been deeply damaged beyond repair. When we hear about responsibility, we might ask ourselves: "How can I be responsible for past negative experiences, for things I went through, for example, when I was a child?" But that's not the point. Whether or not we're responsible for what happened in the past doesn't change the fact that there is no option to change it now. What's past has gone, it doesn't exist anymore, and no-one can change the past. So there's no point in beating ourselves up.

On the other hand, there is something very important that we can do right now: decide that we don't want to let the past dictate our life any longer, that we want to turn the page and start afresh. It may not be very pleasant to hear, but the truth is that the only thing holding us to the past is our willingness to remain stuck in it. It's up to us to take the decisive step to go from powerless victim to responsible creator of our own life. No one can stop us from doing this, but no one can do it for us.

Some of us think that, in order to free ourselves from the past, we need to analyse in detail everything that has happened, until we confirm that we are not to blame for being who we are. It was our upbringing, our family environment, the fact that our father or mother didn't love us as they should have, the fact that we had many siblings or, on the contrary, that we were an only child. Of course, all these things have an influence on who we are, but they are no excuse for not wanting to change.

In fact, if we want to go down that road, we can't be satisfied with understanding how our parents' dysfunctions gave rise to ours. We would be assuming that we are the result of what they were, but they, in turn, chose to be that way. If we're going to follow this path, then we must investigate what made them the way they were and, probably, what made our grandparents behave the way they did. In fairness, we'd have to go back in time, generation after generation, to the beginning of humanity.

I don't know if it needs to be so complicated. If understanding the genesis of some of our dysfunctions helps us to gain distance and heal them, so much the better. But the only advantage I recognise in this approach is that it makes it easier for us to understand that what we are today is due to a set of past causes and circumstances. We can't change them, but if this is true, then we can create other causes and circumstances now and thus change the future.

Freeing ourselves from guilt

It's essential to realise the difference between responsibility and guilt. Exaggerated, almost pathological, guilt is one of the great plagues of the West, something of which Easterners are generally unaware. It is not just a vague cultural inheritance, largely the result of our Judeo-Christian heritage; it's something some of us are engulfed in constantly.

For us to feel guilty, we must have harmed or caused suffering to someone through our actions. This is a normal and entirely desirable process, an awareness of the harmful nature of our actions. We then feel regret: we wish we could go back and change our behaviour; we wish we had never made that mistake in the first place. This too is healthy and necessary. It's what happens next that makes the difference. The pathological process of guilt gets stuck there, speculating endlessly. If I hadn't said those words; if I had arrived earlier; if I hadn't been so irritable, if I hadn't been drinking... none of that would have happened. We want at all costs to change what can't be changed, to erase our mistakes, or turn back time. And because that's not possible, we get stuck.

Hidden in guilt is sometimes the inability to accept that we too can make mistakes. As we always want to be right and believe that only others make mistakes, it can be difficult to recognise that, like any other human being, we too can make bad decisions. It may not be easy to face up to this reality, but it's a necessary step towards freeing ourselves from guilt.

However, the fact that we regret something we've done is a very good sign. It means that we've probably changed, gained wisdom, learnt something. The person we were when we committed the faux pas no longer exists plus, through ignorance, inexperience or suffering, we understand that we acted differently at that time than we would have done today. We did our best and, even if it was a mistake, regretting it forever doesn't change the course of things. If there is anything we can do to improve or correct the current situation, we should do it. We can apologise to those we have hurt in some way, but we can't force them to accept our apologies. It may be that they are not yet ready for this reconciliation—we must respect them and give them the time they need. On the other hand, we don't have to wait for their forgiveness to move on. We accept the consequences of our actions—including the fact that others won't forgive us—and we learnt our lesson. We recognise that what we did was wrong, we are sure that we don't want to hurt or harm someone in the same way again in the future, and we resolutely decide to change our behaviour.

If it's not possible to correct the situation we created, we can simply do positive acts of an opposite nature to the harm we've done. Not as a form of atonement or punishment, thinking: "I made someone suffer so now I have to pay", but as an antidote to the negative energy generated. Helping someone, being generous, showing affection or offering protection is good for both the receiver and the giver. There are no downsides.

If we've been living with guilt for a long time, we may not be able to let go of it all at once. After we've taken all these steps, if we still feel guilty from time to time, we should repeat to ourselves: "I've recognised my mistake and I've done everything I can to improve the situation. There's no benefit in continuing to feel guilty. I must let go." We then move on. We shouldn't let ourselves dwell in negative feelings that serve no purpose and bring no benefit, and just accept that we're just like anyone else, liable to make mistakes, but make a strong decision not to commit the same mistake again. Then, the important next step is to actually change our behaviour. When we feel the joy of being useful to others and help them, we can recognise how making mistakes has made us a better, more conscientious and attentive person. We can then rejoice.

If our guilt persists despite everything we've said above, then it's probably because it is a deeply engrained habit. When we feel guilty, we should try to find out what we are feeling guilty about. Did we behave in a way that hurt someone? Did we make a mistake? Have we harmed anyone? In cases of chronic guilt, we may be surprised to find nothing really serious to justify it. It's just a persistent, habitual feeling that, because we've never looked into it, we've always felt was justified. But even if we do find a valid reason, we should follow the steps detailed above until we can accept it and move on. We should also bear in mind that regretting things we cannot change will achieve no purpose whereas committing to positive intentions and actions and becoming a better human being brings goodness to the world.

It is sometimes essential to realise that we are not responsible for all the emotional reactions people may have. When people overreact, blaming it on us, we have to be able to discern how far our responsibility goes and what we can no longer be blamed for. If somebody tells us "If you leave me, I will drink myself to death", for example, we must be clear about the fact that drinking him or herself to death is a choice and not a direct consequence of our actions. Taking things that far is their responsibility, not ours. Talking to someone impartial can help us see things more clearly. And we should always remember that each of us is responsible for his or her own choices and reactions.

Being gentle with ourselves

It's curious to note that, despite Buddhism's deep understanding of human psychology, self-esteem problems seem to be totally alien to it. It's not a doctrinal prejudice: in general, I think it was an unknown problem in Eastern culture. We must recognise that, even in the West, it's a recent concept. When I was a kid, nobody talked about self-esteem. There were certainly people who didn't like themselves, or felt confident, but there was no word for it at that time.

It's not true that we don't like ourselves. Deep down we continue to look after our own interests above anyone else's, even if we don't realise it. What we have is an unfavourable opinion of what we believe we are compared to what we think—or what others think—we should be. We then feel a mixture of resentment and wounded pride for not living up to our own and other people's expectations.

It happens in families that parents can compare and belittle their children. "You're not like your brother; you don't do anything right; you can't be trusted with anything..." It's clear that these kinds of statements, heard over and over again, don't make us feel confident and predispose us to constantly evaluate ourselves. But, even if we're angry with our parents for the rest of our lives, we can't go back and erase what they said. Therefore, there's no point in wanting them to realise or apologise—they might do so, but there's every chance that it will never happen. They simply think they were trying to get us to make an effort because they loved us and wanted the best for us.

What may really be helpful is to realise that it's not really about liking or disliking ourselves but rather liking or disliking our *image* of ourselves. Such feelings are based on judgements and comparisons and there is not much kindness involved. Chances are that we are equally unsympathetic towards others and more judgemental than understanding. In such cases, no doubt a psychological approach has its role to play and can be extremely useful. Sometimes we have such a dysfunctional ego and such a degree of self-hatred that we really need to replace the negative image with a positive one. The help of a psychotherapist can be indispensable for us to be able to function as human beings. But we can also take a slightly different route, realise that this is a false issue and start establishing a different kind of relationship with ourselves.

We should take time to observe ourselves without judgement. Meditation develops this kind of attention and trains us to be simple, relaxed spectators. We can observe things like breathing, sounds or sensations, without judgement or opinion. If we learn to relax in this way for a few minutes a day we can get in touch with our inner world in a different way. I'll explain more about how to meditate later, and at the end of the book you'll find exercises you can do yourself.

Instead of reproaching our faults and weaknesses, we should realise that we don't have to be more or less than anyone else and recognise that, because we are like everyone else, we can feel fear, anxiety and anger. Instead of judging our emotions, we should just recognise them. This doesn't mean we should let them rule us, but instead of judging or ignoring them, we can just recognise and agree to deal with them. No matter how scary or ugly they are, they are no worse or better than anyone else's, and they can be transformed.

When we accept to look at these emotions instead of rejecting them, we'll discover that they hide old wounds, resentments and scars. We may need to talk about them, release them, accept and understand them. If we can depend on the advice of a confidant, a mentor, a therapist or a spiritual friend, to listen without judgement, we should take that step and find someone who can help us gain perspective on what has happened, without blaming ourselves or anyone else.

It may seem impossible, at this point, that we will ever be able to let go of these old wounds. That's because, for now, we reject or condemn them and would like to make them disappear. But when we start to relax and accept them, those old tensions rise to the surface like air bubbles trapped in the bottom of a bottle. The process produces a feeling of liberation and triumph that will make us feel more confident and self-assured.

Realising that, as we've seen, we are all trying to do our best helps the process of forgiving ourselves and others. Depending on the case, it can be difficult to let go and forgive someone who has hurt us deeply. Forgiveness can't be forced; we will have to take our time. If we continue the process of acceptance and release, we'll see that, when we least expect it and in a totally natural way, forgiveness will emerge, filling us with immense compassion and gratitude. Whenever we are confronted with a situation that we associate with a painful memory, we will begin to notice that it no longer has the same impact. The pain remains, but the predominant feeling is "I'm no longer the person who lived through that experience". This is absolutely true.

Little by little, we'll start to be gentler with ourselves. Instead of constantly judging ourselves, we start to enjoy our own company. We don't live so much on comparisons: we're not more, we're not less. The point is not to love instead of hating ourselves—we start to feel love, we start to *be* love. And that love extends to everything and everyone, including ourselves.

Even if we think the most important thing is to look after others, we do have to look after ourselves first, our physical, mental, emotional and even financial health. If we're not in balance and in good health, how can we look after anyone else? Some people feel they should put the interests and needs of others before their own. This can be a deeply altruistic attitude, but more often than not it's an unconscious strategy to be accepted or loved.

We can tell one from the other by noticing how it makes us feel. If it's true altruism, the result can only make us feel happy. But if it's a desire to be accepted, loved or recognised, we'll end up noticing some frustration, a feeling of not being recognised or respected as much as we'd like, no matter how much we do. Ultimately, to get others to respect us, we should start by respecting ourselves.

Furthermore, we'll see in one of the next chapters how true altruism is different from the need to give meaning to our lives through others. We often think that we must give in to everything, self-sacrifice and almost lose ourselves to be good fathers, good mothers or good husbands or wives. But what drives us, in general, is more fear and attachment than a selfless desire for the other person to be happy. Therefore, to truly love others, we must love ourselves and enjoy our own company. We have to rely mainly on ourselves in order to not be overly dependent so that we can offer our friendship selflessly and without expectations.

Developing awareness

The main tool to accomplish inner transformation is awareness. If we're not aware of our actions, words and thoughts we cannot transform them. This kind of attention is something very open and has nothing to do with control. People who are very controlling are always measuring and evaluating their behaviour so as not to allow themselves to go overboard or show weaknesses, and we might think that this is the kind of awareness we are talking about. But it's not. The mindfulness we need to develop comes from an open and relaxed attitude of full awareness and not from paranoid, controlling vigilance. It's not about evaluating our behaviour, punishing ourselves or feeling guilty. Mindfulness is a simple observation of what is happening in us and around us. It is not a state of judgement but a state of full awareness and has four main focuses: mindfulness of the body; mindfulness of feelings; mindfulness of the states of mind and mindfulness of what is happening around us.

Mindfulness of the body consists of being aware of our body, its posture, physical sensations but also the actions we are taking. Noticing what is happening on a physical level and correcting it–if necessary–but without judgement. Yoga, Tai-Chi, Qigong, walking meditation and other meditative physical exercises are excellent for training this type of mindfulness, but we can train ourselves while doing any task such as doing the washing up, preparing dinner, vacuuming the house or gardening. By developing this kind of awareness, we become more present in our actions and make less mistakes. We become more mindful of our gestures and movements and are more likely to know where we dropped our keys or where we left our glasses.

Mindfulness of feelings allows us to be aware of the feelings of attraction, repulsion or indifference that arise. In the absence of this kind of mindfulness, we give rise unwillingly to feelings that only bring us distress. A simple discomfort can grow into impatience, irritation and finally an outburst of anger, with all the internal and external consequences that follow, simply because we didn't realise the process and didn't address it in time.

Mindfulness of moods allows us to be aware of our mental attitude at any given moment. When we are aware of them, we automatically distance ourselves and don't get caught up in them so easily. A state of mind is always only temporary, something that can change very easily, as long as we don't cling to it. The more we become aware of our moods, the more independent we become and the less they control us.

Finally, being mindful to what's going on around ußs allows us to be fully present where we are. When we talk to someone, take part in a meeting or are with family, we are not semi-absent, lost in thought, immersed in our phones and messages. We will notice the little clues people inadvertently give about how they are thinking or feeling and can respond appropriately. Paying attention to what's going on will also allow us to enjoy the small details that we usually miss and that are essential to living fully.

The state we are usually in is only semi-conscious. Of course, we're aware of what's going on, but only in the background. Most of our attention is absorbed by the thoughts and other mental processes taking place in the foreground. Mindful awareness makes a significant change in our state of presence, giving us an increased ability to remain in and enjoy the present moment in any situation in life.

Familiarising with Meditation

As we are much more used to letting our thoughts drift away, this kind of attention is new to us. There's nothing mysterious or esoteric about it, nothing we don't already have the ability to do. A nature lover may silence the thinking mind while walking in the forest or planting flowers in the garden; a sportsman while practising their sport; a musician while playing an instrument; a craftsman while developing their art. Meditation allows us to train this attention in a very simple and direct way, and this is accessible to everyone.

In our habitual state, thoughts follow one another in an uninterrupted flow. Although there are visual thoughts, most of the time we have the sensation of a voice inside us that is punctuating, commenting and directing. This discursive thought captures most of our attention in such a way that we are often lost in thought and totally oblivious to what we are doing. Throughout life we have developed chains of thought that always lead us to the most habitual places in our minds. Memories of the past and projections of the future keep us absent from the present moment, locked in the mind's cinema room where our favourite films play continuously. This intense mental activity consumes a large part of our energy and is also the source of much of our anguish. There is a fundamental difference between being afraid when we see a lion and being afraid when we think we might see a lion. In our current experience, the sight of a lion in the wild is very unlikely. On the other hand, we might be terrified at the thought of seeing a lion an unlimited number of times a day. And there lies our problem. As we are immersed in the virtual experience of our mind 24 hours a day, we suffer the terrors and anxieties of everything it can imagine and not just the fears of the physical situations we face. The overwhelming majority of our suffering is mental and has nothing to do with a concrete, immediate situation.

Meditation is training ourselves to shift our attention from thinking to something that is happening here and now, like our breathing, sensations or sounds, for example. By training in this way, we can become much more aware and gain freedom from our thoughts. We don't have to fight them or follow them anymore, we can just relax and let them pass as clouds blown by the wind.

A description of the recommended posture and straightforward instructions for meditation can be found at the end of the book. We can start with meditating for a few minutes—we shouldn't make it too long. It's important that it becomes an enjoyable time, or we'll soon tire of it. There will be a lot of thoughts, and we may even get the impression that we have more thoughts than usual. That's not true: we've just become more aware of them.

The benefits of meditation manifest quicker in everyday life than during the sessions. Even after many years of practice there will always be some days where our mind seems restless. However, with very little training, people often find that meditation allows them to distance themselves from situations and respond better rather than reacting in the usual way.

Devoting a few moments a day to meditation means spending some time in our own company, which can be daunting for some. But it's a practically indispensable complement to a fulfilled life.

Learning from mistakes

One of the costs of living on autopilot is that we constantly repeat the same mistakes. When we want to start living in a more conscious way, we absolutely need the detachment that meditation brings about. Thanks to it, we can become aware of what we are doing, what we are feeling, what is going on, and we gain the freedom from our habitual patterns. But you have to be prepared to accept that this process is slow and progressive. It is very common for people who start down this path to be thrilled when they realise that they've made progress, that they realise their mistakes much more quickly. But they can also become discouraged when they realise all the attitudes they still haven't managed to change.

The American actress and writer Portia Nelson wrote this poem entitled "There's a hole in my sidewalk[3]" which expresses this process very well:

---

[3] There's a Hole in My Sidewalk: The Romance of Self-Discovery is the title of the book.

GROW YOUR OWN HAPPINESS

Chapter One
I walk down the street.
There is a deep hole in the sidewalk.
I fall in.
I am lost… I am helpless.
It isn't my fault.
It takes forever to find a way out.

Chapter Two
I walk down the same street.
There is a deep hole in the sidewalk.
I pretend I don't see it.
I fall in again.
I can't believe I am in the same place.
But it isn't my fault.
It still takes a long time to get out.

Chapter Three
I walk down the same street.
There is a deep hole in the sidewalk.
I see it is there.
I still fall in… it's a habit.
My eyes are open.
I know where I am.
It is my fault… I get out immediately.

Chapter Four
I walk down the same street.

There is a deep hole in the sidewalk.
I walk around it.

Chapter Five
I walk down another street.

The first stage is total unconsciousness. We didn't see the hole; we didn't realise the situation–because we were distracted–and so we don't know how we fell in. We are hurt and it's not our fault, we don't know where we are, there's nothing we can do. It's very difficult to find a way out because we spend a lot of time making excuses for ourselves, looking for culprits and protesting. We are entirely victims of the situation.

In the second stage there's a slight improvement: we see the hole! Of course, we pretend we didn't and fall in once more. After we have fallen in, we can't believe we are here again, but it's not our fault. Why hasn't the council filled in the hole yet? We are still not ready to take responsibility and we still think we are a victim.

Even though we can clearly see the hole, we still fall in the third time. However, we are now fully aware that we could have avoided it, that we fell in out of habit because we weren't quick enough. We are fully aware that we are responsible, and we'll be out in a flash.

In the fourth stage we learnt our lesson. We follow the same path as always, but we pass next to the hole. We've finally gained some distance and some freedom. Falling into the hole is perfectly useless, it doesn't benefit anyone. You might think that just walking past the hole would be enough. But no. In the last stage we take a different path. We've changed radically.

Gaining awareness is a process that is achieved by repeating mistakes. Making mistakes is never a problem if it allows us to learn a lesson. So we shouldn't get discouraged and keep trying.

Don't make excuses

Excuses are the lies we tell ourselves to avoid dealing with the truths that bother us. The problem is that as long as we turn our heads so as not to see reality, we continue to dodge the issues. One of the most important steps in the process of personal transformation is to look at who we are without complacency, but with compassion, awareness and courage. In this process of change, most of us must face our own inertia and resistance. Change is difficult and can be uncomfortable at first. That's why, even when we think we want to change, a less conscious part of us comes up with a thousand excuses for why it is impossible.

One of the most common excuses for not making the changes we want in our lives is that we don't have time. When we hear ourselves say this, we must recognise that it's not true. The truth is that whatever we think we don't have time for, isn't important enough for us. If it were, we'd make time for it. Every day we find time for insignificant things like watching TV, reading magazines, going on social media etc. If it were really for lack of time, then we wouldn't have time for all that either. Of course, we're often much more motivated to do things that relax and distract us than to reflect or meditate. Therefore, we need to be very clear about the importance of personal transformation. Once we are fully decided, we'll find the time, even if we have to reorganise our priorities.

Another common excuse is thinking that we're not capable, that it's not for us. We think of it as a lack of confidence, whereas in reality it's just inertia and laziness. The more we hear about the spiritual path, the more we realise that it's not a quick fix–it requires work and application. So instead of recognising that we're not up for it, we say we're not capable.

There are also those who think they can't change because they don't have the material means to do so. We could argue that obtaining information or knowledge requires money to buy books, attend lectures and courses. This is partly true. But if we really want to learn, we can borrow a book or search the internet. Especially after the pandemic, we can find online an incredible amount of Buddhist teachings. It is also possible to ask to take part in seminars and retreats in exchange for services or at a reduced price. Almost all Buddhist centres, despite having their own expenses, agree to provide access to information free of charge. Many of them also have a library that you can consult. Ultimately, even if you've only heard a piece of advice or two, what really matters is putting it into practice. Changing your attitude doesn't cost a cent.

It often happened that people wrote to our centre saying they would love to attend a workshop or course but couldn't afford it. We always answered saying they were welcome at no expense, because money shouldn't be an issue. However, almost invariably these people never turned up, therefore showing that perhaps the real issue wasn't money.

We shouldn't let excuses win. We should recognise them for what they are and replace them with the truth. Instead of saying "I don't have time", we should say "I am not willing to make the time";

instead of saying "I'm not capable", we should say "I'm not willing to make the effort". Curiously, when we finally manage to face the truth, we'll be ready to grow, and all the obstacles will disappear as if by magic.

It's easy to blame external and uncontrollable factors such as lack of time, information or means. But as long as we use these excuses, we're shirking responsibility and preventing ourselves from seeing the real issues behind them. We can't increase the number of hours in the day, but we can organise our tasks according to priorities and choose where we are going to apply our time and energy. If our material resources are scarce, we can prioritise how we use them and find creative solutions. If we are patient and humble, we will always be able to learn something.

Avoiding complaints

Constantly feeling negative means that we tend to express ourselves by complaining. We complain that the weather is hot, but if it cools down, we complain that it's cold; we complain about the rain or the lack of it; we complain that life is expensive; that the government doesn't do what it should. We complain about our husband or wife, our children, our colleagues, our friends... Everything can be a cause for complaint for those who focus on the negative.

Complaining expresses and reinforces a state of dissatisfaction that keeps us powerless and unhappy. Every time we complain, we feel bad. If we complain about what's happening—because the driver in front of us is going slowly, for example—we express our disagreement with the present moment and clench ourselves into a position of resistance. If we complain about something that has happened, we relive it again, deepening its mark on us. But, logically speaking, if it was a bad experience, why would we want to repeat it again and again?

Complaining doesn't solve anything; it just predisposes us to feeling unhappy and frustrated. Sometimes you may notice that the people who complain the most are the ones who do the least to change the situations that cause them discomfort. Perhaps they expect others to pay attention to them, but if you're in this category, don't be fooled. Most people aren't at all interested in listening to our complaints and those who do often do so only to get us to listen to theirs.

Observe yourself. Not in an obsessive or controlling way, but simply be more attentive: Do you complain a lot? How do you feel when you complain? How do people react to your complaints? How do you react to other people's complaints? It's important to realise that pointing out something that isn't right isn't necessarily a complaint. Pointing out, with constructive intent, a mistake or something that needs to be corrected, then addressing it to someone who can correct it, is normal and practical.

Talking about a difficult situation isn't necessarily a complaint either. Sometimes we need to share what we're going through in order to find new perspectives or relieve the pressure. In that case, we usually turn to a friend, a trusted person or someone whose opinion we respect, and confide in them. If we have observed how we feel when we complain, we will realise that the energy generated by constructive criticism or venting is not the same as that generated by complaint.

Will Bowen[4], the founder of the *Complaint Free World* movement, has come up with a cunning way to help people kick the habit. On his online site, he offers rubber wristbands to put on your wrist. The idea is to change it the other wrist every time you complain. When you manage to keep it on the same wrist for 21 days in a row, you've lost the habit. This is because, according to psychologists, 21 days is the time it takes to lose a habit. Sounds like a short time... but how many months will it take until you can keep the bracelet on your wrist for 21 days?

If you want to try it out, you don't necessarily have to order the bracelet. You can use any bracelet or ring that is easy to change hands and that you can feel–so you don't forget it easily. The gesture of changing them is very important because it marks the acknowledgement of the complaint with a neutral action and not with disapproval or guilt.

All you need to do is observe yourself. Don't judge. Don't condemn. Observe yourself as if you were someone looking in from the outside, a scientist conducting a study. When you see that you've been complaining all day, don't blame yourself. Recognise the fact and affirm your decision to stop the habit.

Many people ask whether non-verbalised thoughts count as complaints. It's obvious that thoughts also make us feel bad, but for now we should limit ourselves to verbalised complaints. Controlling what we say is difficult enough: controlling what we think is, for the time

---

[4] Will Bowen is the founder of the non-profit organisation Complaint Free World, Inc., which distributes free anti-complaint bracelets and other materials designed to help people make positive changes in their lives.

being, impossible. However, as everything is connected, once we've managed to eliminate the voiced complaints, we can be sure that the negative thoughts will have diminished considerably.

During the first few days we may be terrified by the number of complaints. Sometimes the training begins when we realise that, contrary to what we thought, we do complain a lot. If this is the case, we shouldn't be discouraged or blame ourselves but instead be happy that we've finally realised it and stand firm in our decision to change this habit.

Change what we can–live with the rest

Eliminating complaints from our lives isn't just about stifling them. We must distinguish useless complaints from discomfort generated by something that needs to be addressed and actively take responsibility for any necessary change. In fact, faced with what bothers us, we have only two things to do: change what can be changed and learn to live with what cannot.

If there are things in our life that we don't like, we should change what we can, instead of doing nothing and just complain. When we get cold at night, we often curl up instead of getting out of bed and fetching another blanket. Because we don't want to face the cold for a minute or two, we sleep badly all night. Sometimes we do the same with our lives and live a diminished life instead of changing what isn't right. We probably won't be able to change everything we think is wrong with our life overnight. The important thing is to start somewhere. We can start with the most urgent or the easiest. Just start!

When it comes to things that can't be changed, we should learn to look at them differently. We live in a world where there are always problems, difficulties and setbacks. Nothing is perfect. But also, as Shakespeare said, "Nothing is good or bad in itself, we make it so." This gives us responsibility but also freedom. There are things we can't change—but we can change the way they make us feel.

If we are always emphasising the unpleasant aspects of someone, we'll condition ourselves to hate them more and more and feel unhappy because we can't avoid them. Conversely, if we emphasise the positive aspects, we'll start to recognise some of their qualities and feel better. Even if we don't get to like them, we can at least feel less aversion. Nothing and no-one in this world is completely good or bad. If we learn to recognise the qualities of some of the situations we consider negative, we can accept them better and even make them useful. A little reflection can teach us to see adverse situations in a different light.

Here's a funny story that illustrates this point. It takes place in India where, even more than in Europe, relations between daughters-in-law and mothers-in-law are problematic. There, when girls get married, they go to live with their in-laws and are often oppressed by their mothers-in-law.

The story is of a newly married girl whose relationship with her mother-in-law was very bad. Her mother-in-law was very demanding and never missed an opportunity to correct and humiliate her. She, in turn, didn't take kindly to the comments, got upset and relations between the two were very tense. The conflict escalated to such an extent that one day, after a particularly heated exchange of words, the girl left the house in a fury, determined to put an end to the situation. Whilst walking down the street aimlessly, she passed an apothecary's shop and thought she had found the solution to her problem: she was going to poison her mother-in-law.

She then went into the shop and asked for some poison. The apothecary asked her what it was for, and she explained the situation. The apothecary then fetched a small bottle containing a greenish liquid and told her: "All you have to do is put three drops in your mother-in-law's food at lunch and dinner. The poison has no taste, so she won't notice. It takes a while to take effect, so it's only when the bottle is finished that the dose ingested is fatal."

The girl paid and, as she was about to leave the shop, the apothecary asked, "I see you are young and inexperienced, can I give you some advice?" "Yes, of course," she replied "What you want is to live in peace with your husband, don't you? But if your relationship with his mum is so bad, it's possible that people will suspect you, the moment she becomes ill and dies. To avoid this, it would be best to change your attitude towards her from now on. Don't respond when she's unpleasant, do everything she asks without grumbling, treat her as if she were your mother. That way, no-one will get suspicious."

The girl found the advice very wise, thanked him and left. From then on, she followed the apothecary's advice and began to treat her mother-in-law with the utmost respect and solicitude. She obeyed her in everything and was all smiles and kindness. Seeing the change in her daughter-in-law, the mother-in-law thought "This girl isn't unfriendly after all!" and began to treat her a little better. The girl, in turn, being treated better, became even kinder. Soon relations between the two improved and there began to be a good understanding.

When the bottle was almost empty, the girl panicked. Her mother-in-law's death was imminent, and she no longer wanted her to die. In those weeks she had discovered that she could be a good and kind person and had learnt to love her. In tears, she returned to the chemist.

"I need you to sell me the antidote to the poison I gave my mother-in-law. I hope it's not too late! I can see now that she's a good person and I can't think of her dying because of me."

The apothecary smiled. "Don't worry. What I sold you was just an extract of harmless herbs. I knew that if you followed my advice, you'd change your mind."

All positive situations have drawbacks, and all negative situations have qualities. What's more, an apparently negative situation can protect us from greater danger, while a positive situation can expose us to painful consequences. As in the story, once we stop battling circumstances and learn to become friends with them, we can transform our experience completely and learn to like what we previously disliked.

Feeling grateful

In modern society we often have the impression that everything can be bought or sold. The fact that objects and services are paid for leads us to develop a false sense of autonomy, forgetting that behind them are people. We have the pretence of thinking that we don't need anything or anyone because we are perfectly capable of subsisting on our own. As well as being false, this idea is also harmful, reducing mutual help to a mere transaction, cultivating hostile indifference as a basic mode of interaction and definitively killing any chance of gratitude towards other human beings.

On the other hand, because we spend more time focussing on what we don't have; it's rare for us to be grateful for everything we already have, such as health, affection, friendship or money. So we can't even let the best things in life make us happy: while we have them, we take them for granted; when we lose them, we are devastated because we suddenly discover how essential they were. However, it is possible to change this ungrateful and dissatisfied state of mind by thinking differently.

In my parents' generation, people used to feel very grateful when someone did something for them. Nowadays we don't think we have to feel grateful because people just did their duty or their job. We are more likely to find fault or think they could have done more, than to appreciate what they did for us. We are often under the impression that gratitude is a feeling that will benefit others, and so we're sparing with it—we're not going to hand out more gratitude than people deserve! However, we are completely wrong: we may never tell someone how grateful we are, but it would make us feel immensely good. So don't miss an opportunity and start training yourself now.

When talking about gratitude, traditional texts use as an example the gratitude we naturally feel towards our parents. In the modern world, such a feeling can seem obsolete. Many people are of the opinion that their parents could have done more or been better–

especially since all our difficulties have been blamed on childhood trauma.

However incompetent our parents may have been, at least they raised us and generally tried to do the best they could, based on their own experiences and knowledge. Contrary to what we think, it's not compulsory for parents to love their children, or to raise and educate them. Many mothers abandon their children because they don't want to or are unable to raise them. And if we were adopted, instead of being hurt that our biological parents didn't want us (and we usually don't know their reasons), we can focus on gratitude for those who, under no obligation to do so, took us in, brought us up and loved us all our lives.

Following this train of thought, we can extend our gratitude to family members, teachers, friends, colleagues and so on, to all the people who have helped and inspired us, in whatever way. Regardless of their intentions or qualities, what they did for us was decisive and fundamental. Even enemies or people who harm us sometimes play a crucial role in our lives. It's not unreasonable to be grateful to them too.

At the end of this book you'll find a guided meditation on gratitude you can use to condition yourself not only to feel less tormented, but frankly happier. Although your priority may simply be to free yourself from negative thoughts and emotions, the most effective and quickest method is to replace them with positive ones.

Someone told me that he had found a way to promote gratitude. He found a pebble, a soft round pebble like the kind you find on beaches and started carrying it around in his pocket. At the end of each day, when he took the pebble from his pocket and again in the morning when he picked up the pebble, he remembered to feel grateful for something. During the day, if he put his hand in his pocket and felt the stone, he would do the same exercise. The stone of gratitude, as he called it, became a precious tool in his transformation. Finally, when the attitude became habitual, he gave it to a friend.

Keeping a gratitude diary

To make this practice more consistent, I often recommend keeping a gratitude diary, i.e. starting to write down in a notebook all the things you feel grateful for. If gratitude isn't exactly your predominant feeling, you may not find something to write down straight away. Don't give up. Even if you can only think of difficult things, think about how many people have much worse things in life and feel grateful. So, in the worst case, you can start your diary with phrases like "I feel grateful that this or that situation isn't worse".

When we start to see positive things to write down, we shouldn't settle for the obvious ones. We should think carefully and review all areas of our life: family, health, profession, money, etc., not just write down a couple of things, but go deeper and think about everything in our life that has brought us to where we are today.

A very common mistake at the beginning is to write what we *think* is important. But having an opinion is not the same as feeling! It's very important that we feel truly grateful for every single thing we write down. The reason we must stop focusing on negative things is because they make us *feel* bad; the reason we're trying to focus on positive things is to *feel* good. Feeling is fundamental.

As we get used to focusing on gratitude, we'll start to remember the smallest things. We'll start to feel grateful for a sunny day, a smile from a stranger, a cool breeze on a hot day. When our notebook is well filled, while continuing to add things, we can start to elaborate on the ones we've already written down. List all the positive aspects we find in the various areas of our life. We can complete sentences such as: "I'm very lucky to have good relationships with…" "to have friends who…" "I'm very lucky that my health is…" etc. And we should remember to feel everything we write.

If we commit to adding something to our list every day the results will pay off. Day after day, we'll start to feel grateful for everything we have and we'll feel happier and happier. We can also reflect on things of a general nature that affect our life. Here are some examples of such things, which we generally take for granted, but which are really privileges not given to all human beings.

The fact that you're reading this book proves that we were both lucky enough to be born at a time and in a situation where we could learn to read and write. Even today, that's an opportunity not given to everyone! We live in a time and place where we have access to information and knowledge like never before. Where, for many, many years, we have had freedom of opinion, expression and assembly. Where we can practise any religion, where we enjoy constitutional freedoms and guarantees.

We women can also add the fact that today we enjoy the right to vote and a legally identical status to men. This is probably the first time in recent human history that women have enjoyed such a status. Generally, we live in countries that are not at war and where we enjoy great security, are protected from natural disasters and benefit from a climate without regular catastrophes.

Even the richest people, just a few decades ago, didn't have a tenth of the comforts we enjoy today. No running water, no basic sanitation and even less electricity, television, telephone, internet... Not so long ago, computers, mobile phones and GPS were the stuff of science fiction. Our ancestors would have been amazed at the facilities of modern life: an infinite variety of foodstuffs—from the four corners of the world—in all seasons and at affordable prices; the eradication of diseases and epidemics that used to kill people by the thousands; the use of machines for the heaviest jobs that used to be done by hand; the possibility of travelling to the other side of the planet in just a few hours and communicating instantly with people far away from us.

We can think of the advances in medicine, particularly surgery... The spectacular advances in the treatment of countless diseases and in pain management... All these advances that we tend to take for granted, would have made our ancestors astonished. For them, having just some of what we have today would probably have been synonymous with happiness. It's also true that some of our comfort is excessive and that the planet is suffering. Of course, we must be mindful of the environment and do what we can to respect nature and other life forms, but at this point we are focusing on recognising how lucky we are in the situation we find ourselves.

While considering all this we shouldn't forget that all these comforts are not available to everyone. Only a small fraction of the world's population has access to what we enjoy every day without even realising it.

As Nagarjuna (a 3rd century Indian teacher) suggested, when we wake up in the morning, we should rejoice that we're alive: during the night, many people around the world died. After breathing out, being able to breathe in again is a miracle.

Even the bad things in our lives, whether past or present, have one great quality—they could have been much worse! Whatever has happened to us, the same thing and much worse has happened to someone else. Imagine a scenario much worse than yours; imagine all the consequences of that scenario; imagine what your life would be like in that situation. Now go back to the real situation. How do you feel? I'm sure much better, immensely grateful that things aren't so bad. We can do this exercise for the difficult things in our life. For each demanding situation, we can count the good that remains and rejoice because it could have been much worse.

At this stage, we could start making a list of the bad things that ended up working out well. Sometimes it's the conflict with someone that make us grow, reversals of fortune that push us to change, illnesses or accidents that force us to stop and reorient our lives. Gratitude turns the negative into a positive. If we find a way to feel grateful for our problems, they will turn into blessings.

Being predisposed to gratitude means not taking anything for granted and opening ourselves up to the richness of our surroundings. Gratitude opens the doors to life. It makes what we have more than enough. It turns outrage into acceptance, chaos into order, and confusion into clarity. It turns problems into gifts, failures into successes, unforeseen events into opportunities and mistakes into milestones. With gratitude we make sense of the past, bring peace to the present and create a vision for the future.

TSERING PALDRON

Feeling the contentment

By feeling more and more grateful for what we have, we open our hearts and predispose ourselves to appreciate life. Naturally, as we learn to value more what we have, we also begin to feel a greater sense of satisfaction.

Many people think that contentment is counterproductive. If all of us were happy with what we have, there would be no progress and no ambition, they say. We'd be fine with whatever we had and wouldn't make the slightest effort to improve. Obviously, that's not what this is about. Feeling grateful and happy with what we have doesn't mean that we can't improve and that we have to abandon any goals. It does mean that, instead of making happiness conditional on achieving something, we choose to be happy now, with what we have.

Dissatisfaction is a state of mind that doesn't change when we get what we want. Normally, when we have this state of mind, as soon as we get what we set out for, we want something else, and we feel dissatisfied again. Whether we have a lot or a little, we can always feel dissatisfied, as happens with extremely wealthy people who have everything that ordinary mortals can only dream of.

Like dissatisfaction, contentment is also a state of mind. Instead of feeling dissatisfied we can feel content, whether we have everything we dreamed of or not. Contentment is achieved when we appreciate what we have and value it. That's not to say that it isn't possible to improve our situation–or that we shouldn't do what we can to do so–but we must never detract from the happiness we already feel.

When we manage to stay more in the present moment, without getting lost in the intricacies of the past and the apprehensions of the future, the thousand and one little things of the present are factors of fulfilment and well-being. We often think that only very important events can bring us happiness, but the smell of wet soil, the light of a sunny day, the flavour of a delicious dish, an hour spent with friends, or a good laugh are all little things that fill our day with joy.

Building a refuge

Some children like to have a sanctuary, usually a small space where they can hide and feel safe. I remember my favourite spot very well, behind a sofa in a corner at my parents' house. We adults also need a refuge. It can be a physical space, an area in a room in the house, a shed at the bottom of the garden, but essentially, it's an inner space, a feeling of comfort and security that arises through a memory, a sensation or an activity.

For example, on a rainy day, sitting on the sofa with a blanket on your legs, a fire in the fireplace and a good book can give you a feeling of comfort. Eventually, simply thinking about it can have the same effect. We can find our internal refuge in a memory, a thought, a feeling, wherever we like, but the most important thing is to cultivate it, in other words, to think about it regularly, to let it settle in a corner of our mind, like a beautiful painting that we bring into our home and like to contemplate.

Visualisation is now also used by psychotherapists and psychologists to treat their patients. Contrary to what the word suggests, it's not just about *seeing*. In this sense, visualising our living room, for example, is not about being able to describe what is there or mentally construct a detailed image. The aim is to give rise to the sensation of comfort or security that we have when you are in our room, to feel as if we were there. This is a natural ability of our mind that, regrettably, we can use unconsciously to make ourselves feel bad. When we mentally relive a painful situation, for example, we are using this same imaginative capacity but only to torture ourselves unnecessarily.

Meditation is an excellent refuge because it's supposed to be a time when we relax and feel good. Tibetan Buddhism uses visualisations, mantra recitations and other techniques to generate positive feelings such as love, compassion, joy, confidence, etc.

Prayer or internal thoughts are often used as refuges, both by practitioners of the different spiritual paths and by people with no religion. In the last part of the book, I'll explain some simple techniques that can be used by anyone.

But the bottom line is: whatever our refuge is, we have to build it, in other words, we have to devote some time and energy to cultivating the positive feeling it gives us and creating the association. As well as being useful in everyday life, it will be a very precious friend in difficult times.

Cultivating connections

Despite the development of the media and social networks, modern lifestyles lead us to live very isolated from each other. In theory, we are closer to our next-door neighbour than when we lived spread out in large spaces, but in practice we can spend years sharing the same building and never say good morning. On public transport, in queues, in waiting rooms, we look at each other askance, with suspicion, or simply ignore each other. Indifference and passive hostility are gradually becoming the dominant form of interaction between strangers.

Even when it comes to friends and acquaintances, although we're constantly looking at our mobile phones and keeping an eye on social media, this doesn't mean that we cultivate many good friendships. As our way of thinking becomes more and more individualistic and narrow, the possibility of establishing warm relationships with others also fades. Nowadays, friends are strangers with whom we go out, have drinks and try to have a good time, but for whom we are not willing to go out of our way. At the first opportunity, we don't hesitate to dump them if they are ill, or their social situation deteriorates.

Within families, the picture isn't much better. Couples who haven't divorced after three or four years are rare. Children who love, respect and enjoy their parents' company are disappearing, and television has replaced family life. A few years ago, people complained that families had stopped talking when they got together in front of the telly in the evenings. Today, even that is no longer possible: everyone has a television, a computer and an iPad where they can watch their favourite programme or trawl the internet.

However, a life devoid of sincere emotional ties is deeply frustrating and gives us a sense of emptiness and meaninglessness. That's why we can't just wait for others to come to us. We must take the first step, whether we are sure of being welcomed or not.

Obviously, it's not about imposing our presence or our affection, about being nosy and annoying, but about opening up, and accepting others into our lives. There are also many types of emotional bonds, and we don't have to expect everything from our partners, family and friends and be completely closed off and indifferent to others. There are families where people love each other, enjoy socialising and support each other, and others where they don't. That's just the way it is and there's no point in trying to force it to be different.

We can have sincere and warm bonds with friends, neighbours, colleagues, or even people with whom we have a one-off interaction. We don't need to make sure that the person we smile at, help up the stairs or listen to for a few minutes will be in our lives forever. We can enjoy genuine heart-to-heart contact, whether it lasts a minute or several years. In this sense, voluntary work can be very rewarding and enriching. The relationships we establish in this kind of context are much more devoid of expectations than friendship or family relationships. We don't expect people to be there for us and so the love we give and receive is selfless.

I'm part of an organisation that supports terminally ill patients, *Amara,* and I can tell from experience that, although it's something that many people find frightening, being present and giving human warmth to someone in a terminal situation is a privilege. The heartfelt relationship that is established in these moments of truth is far from one-sided: most volunteers say they receive much more than they give.

This is just one example, but there are many support organisations needing volunteers and countless people in need. So, if we're feeling lonely and don't have any emotional ties, we could very well spare a few hours a week to selflessly get involved in something that benefits others. In fact, we can be sure that we will benefit just as much, if not more, than those we support.

Pets, cats and dogs for example, are also an excellent way of bonding. They don't demand anything or charge us; they just give us love and affection in exchange for our attention. What's more, in the case of dogs especially, because we must take them out several times a day, we're forced to get out of the house and do a bit of exercise—which is beneficial to us and the dogs. Finally, while walking our dog, we inevitably end up interacting with other dog owners and make friends with them.

The therapeutic effect of a pet is such that the warden of a prison in the United States decided to allow the prisoners to look after rescue dogs. The results were spectacular: the atmosphere in the prison changed radically, violence decreased, and the prisoners began to interact with each other in a friendlier way.

To feel happy and fulfilled we don't have to find a philosophical meaning to our life: we can give it meaning by making it useful to others.

Do what you can, with what you have

Nkosi Johnson[5], a South African boy who was born with AIDS and died aged 12, was a great activist. During his short life he

---

[5] You can find out more about his story in the book *We Are All the Same* by Jim Wooten. Some of his speeches are on Youtube.

defended the rights of children with AIDS "Do what you can with what you have, in the time you are given and where you are," he said.

But we are mostly unaware, immersed in internal thoughts and conflicts, oblivious to what is going on around us. However, if we were asked what we would like to do to make this world a better place, we would surely think of grandiose things like ending hunger or war, discovering a cure for cancer or AIDS. Nothing less than these great acts seems worthwhile to us. We tend to underestimate the power of small actions: saving an ant's life, showing someone the way, offering a smile to a stranger, preparing a meal, listening attentively and without interrupting... what seems like a tiny act to us can make all the difference to someone's life. If we search our memories, we might remember a moment when a small, helpful gesture someone made towards us eased our pain, helped us make the right decision or had a decisive influence on our state of mind.

A friend of mine told me the following story: one day he was walking from his house to the place where several Buddhist teachings had been taking place for a few days. He was passed by a car driven by a gentleman he had seen in previous sessions and, although he had never spoken to him, he waved and smiled at him.

The next day the gentleman came to meet him in the teaching tent. "I've come to thank you," he said, taking his hands in his with effusion. "Thank me? But what for?" my friend asked in surprise. "That smile from yesterday. You know, I'd just had some terrible news and I wanted to end my life. But your smile changed my mind. I can't tell you how grateful I am!"

We can never know the impact of our smallest actions, not least because we rarely get feedback from others. But remember that just a simple smile or act of kindness can open doors, break down barriers and change lives.

Feeling the happiness

Rick Hanson, an American neuropsychologist and author of the book *Buddha Brain,* says that the human brain is like Velcro when it comes to negative feelings and Teflon when it comes to positive ones. When something angers or hurts us, we spend a lot of time mentally revisiting what happened, feeling the pain, anxiety or fear over and over again, but when something pleasant happens, we simply let the experience fade away. Often, we only think back to the happy times we had when we've lost what made us happy, such as at the end of a relationship. And in that case, instead of bringing us happiness, the memory of the good times only brings us pain.

That's why we can't let feelings of happiness evaporate without a trace. We must give them time to penetrate us and leave a positive mark. These moments of happiness can come from the simplest things, such as the joy of arriving home at the end of a working day, the smell of freshly baked bread, the smile of someone we love or the chords of beautiful music. We're all familiar with that feeling that expands our heart, but sometimes we barely give it a few moments.

When we feel a sense of well-being, we should take a moment to appreciate it, dedicate a bit more attention than we normally would and allow ourselves to feel them. If we find that such moments are rare in our present life, we can remember a time in the past when we felt happy. Ideally, we should avoid choosing a moment whose memory is painful for us, as we'll end up doing the opposite of what we're supposed to.

If we like tea, we shouldn't swallow it absent-mindedly but instead savour it. If we enjoy someone's company, we should switch off our mobile phone or place it on silent while we're with them! We miss so many opportunities to feel good about the little things in life because we're inattentive and divided. In the background there's always something else going on, thoughts, problems or simply mental noise. If we try to be present in what we're doing, the moments of well-being and happiness will certainly multiply.

We all aspire to happiness, but often we don't even know how to define it. The most common mistake is to confuse it with pleasure, thus reducing it to something very limited and unstable because pleasure ends quickly—at best with boredom and at worst with pain.

So what makes us happy? On the first level, there are moments of happiness. Lunch with close friends, a good film, a pleasant walk. It's a little more than simple pleasure because it already indicates a certain degree of awareness and appreciation. It's those good moments that we all have in life, but fully appreciated and not lived only as an escape or alienation. Getting drunk to forget our problems or immersing ourselves in television or online games does not count.

What distinguishes these moments of happiness from short term gratification is perhaps the degree of awareness and appreciation, free from clichés. Many people think that drinking champagne in a Jacuzzi, in a five-star hotel in some exotic destination, is happiness.

But it all depends on our level of appreciation. This situation can be boring or even painful, depending on our state of mind.

On the other hand, most people can't really feel the pleasure they can get from experiences, because they live through a mental framework made up of clichés and preconceived ideas. They are actually drinking the *idea* of French champagne–and the price it costs–more than the wine itself and without really enjoying it. They take a photo, post it on social media to show off to friends and think they've made the most of the moment.

So, even to feel the moments of happiness that life offers us, we need to be present and open. A sunny day–completely free of charge–can bring us much more happiness than a stay in a five-star resort. That's why it's not enough to have money to enjoy moments of happiness–we must be able to really appreciate them.

How do we rate our happiness?

Obviously, there are good and bad times in our lives. These fluctuations are part of the nature of things and, even if we had everything we dreamed of, they would still exist. However, some of us take a positive global view of our lives, while others evaluate them negatively. The objective differences can be miniscule.

A Chinese lady was always sad, often crying. One day, someone asked her why. "I have two daughters", she said, "the older one sells rain boots and the younger one sun hats. When it rains, I'm sad for the younger one; when it's sunny, I'm sad for the older one…"

"I have the secret to your happiness," the person said, "it's very simple: when it rains, be happy for your eldest daughter; when it's sunny, be happy for the other one!"

Sometimes we fixate on the things we don't have and feel unhappy, neglecting the countless others we already have and completely losing track of reality. That's why working on gratitude is so essential. For example, one of the greatest assets and also one that we most easily take for granted is our health. When everything is fine and we don't suffer from anything, we don't realise how much our well-being depends on it. It's only when we're suffering from something—and it could even be a simple cold—that we appreciate it. That's why, in order not to take for granted the countless gifts life has given us, we need to reflect more often on how lucky we are. I've often observed how salutary it is to go on a trip to a poor country. We realise first-hand how, by comparison, we live in great abundance and enjoy a truly privileged situation.

When we develop the habit of gratitude, the balance we take of our lives is almost always positive. Even the difficult situations we've experienced are evaluated in terms of the added value they've brought us in terms of learning and life experience.

During an experiment at the University of the State of New York, some subjects were asked to complete the sentence: "I'm glad I'm not..." After a few of these exercises, the subjects felt more satisfied with their lives. Another group of subjects was asked to complete the sentence: "I wish I was…" This time, the experiment provoked a feeling of dissatisfaction. These experiments prove that it is possible to increase or decrease our contentment with life thanks to a change in perspective, and clearly demonstrate the importance of personal judgement in whether or not we feel happy.

The happiness line

It seems that each of us has a capacity to be happy that is much less reliant on external situations than we generally think. Obviously, a positive event can give us a temporary feeling of exhilaration and a setback can lead to a period of despondency, but sooner or later our general sense of well-being tends to return to normal. This principle operates in our daily lives, whether in small everyday incidents or big events. A pay rise, a new car or professional success can put us in a good mood for a moment, but we soon return to our usual level of happiness. In the same way, an argument, a breakdown in the car or any other mishap makes us despair, but after a few hours or days, we forget about it. The same happens in extreme situations of success or crisis. Studies of lottery winners have shown that the initial excitement waned and that, after a while, people returned to their usual level of happiness. Other studies have shown that people who have gone through crisis situations such as serious illness, or losses have found almost the same level of happiness after a period of adaptation. So, if we tend to return to our usual level of happiness whatever the circumstances, what determines that level and, above all, can that level be changed to a higher one?

Some researchers claim that an individual's level of happiness may be, at least in part, genetically determined. Studies carried out on real twins (with the same genetic makeup) show that they tend to have a very similar degree of well-being–regardless of whether they were raised together or not. These studies have led researchers to postulate the existence of a biological level of happiness programmed into the brain at birth.

I remember being maybe sixteen or seventeen when I realised that being happy was a skill I didn't have. I realised that, although I didn't lack anything essential, I was constantly finding reasons to feel bad. Then I wondered if being happy was an innate ability that some people had, and others didn't. Perhaps this realisation of mine had a point after all.

Fortunately for me, I found Buddhism shortly afterwards and never thought about it again. I followed Buddhist training without having happiness as an explicit goal and so I was transformed without realising it. Only now, several decades later, do I realise how my happiness line has changed. Therefore, no matter what the researchers say, I have firsthand proof that this ability may indeed be innate, but it can also be developed and worked on. If you also feel that you're not good at being happy, know that you can change that and learn to live in a much more fulfilling and satisfying way because, above all, happiness is a habit.

Happiness comes from meaning

Ultimately, the most lasting happiness comes from the overall meaning we give to our lives, and this can only come from a goal that not only transcends immediate pleasure, but also our personal well-being. Although, under normal conditions, we value our well-being above all else, in extreme situations the exact opposite can happen. What we wouldn't do for ourselves, we do in the name of values, ideals or other people. This meaning that transcends our personal existence is particularly important in enabling us to get through the ups and downs of life. Only something that is, in our eyes, more important than our own well-being, allows suffering to gain meaning.

In the book *Wind, Sand, and Stars*, Saint-Exupéry tells the story of one of his friends, Guillaumet, who was a pilot. One day his aeroplane was caught in a storm and forced to land in the snows of the Andes. Wrapped in the mailbags he was carrying, he waited 48 hours for the reconnaissance planes to find him, but to no avail. Without food or adequate clothing to protect himself from the cold, his only chance of survival was to walk so as not to freeze to death. He walked for five days and four nights without stopping until, exhausted and almost at the limit of his strength, he slipped and fell. He lacked the ability to carry on and stayed put, tempted to give in to the desire to fall asleep. Letting yourself freeze to death can be tempting in a situation like this because by falling asleep and never waking up he would feel no more pain.

As he began to feel numb, Guillaumet thought of his wife. The insurance would keep her safe from misery. But fallen as he was on a hillside, his body would roll to the bottom of an abyss when the snow melted in spring and he would never be found. He then remembered that, in the event of a disappearance, legal death was only declared after four years and that, until then, his wife would receive nothing. The possibility of his wife being reduced to misery was so unbearable that Guillaumet raised his head: fifty metres ahead he saw a cliff and thought that if he dragged himself there and leaned against it, his body would be found even after the thaw. So, with superhuman effort, he stood up. Once on his feet, Guillaumet walked for another three days and two nights and was finally found and rescued. "What I did, no animal would have done" was his comment. Probably not, and for one crucial reason: an animal can't transcend its self-interest and would probably let himself die.

Our life naturally becomes meaningful when we see it as useful to others. We don't need to have discovered a cure for cancer or have enough money to eradicate world hunger: we just need to feel that we make a difference to the lives of those around us. That's why an altruistic attitude and motivation are so important to us. Contrary to what we generally believe, thinking of others is essentially good for us, as we'll see in the next chapters.

Practical tips from chapter 1:

- Do a few minutes of meditation every day. Start with 5 minutes and gradually increase. During meditation, take short breaks if you feel any tension.
- Keep a gratitude diary. Write down every day the things you feel grateful for, starting with the most obvious. Reflect on the others, the ones you don't normally think about. Finally, also think about the less pleasant situations that made you mature and get to where you are today.
- Choose a refuge: a thought, an image, a feeling that makes you feel confident and relaxed. Meditation is an excellent refuge.

- Prolong moments of happiness by not letting them fade away immediately. Take a few seconds to savour them and, at the end of the day, look back on the best moments.
- Find meaning in your life by being useful to others.

• CHAPTER 2 •

THE CONDITIONS OF WELL-BEING

Whilst happiness can be created regardless of the circumstances, true independence from outer conditions is hard to develop. People with a healthy emotional structure and an innate or acquired ability to feel contentment and happiness get through all of life's situations with ease. A well-trained mind can overcome any circumstances and be scarcely influenced by them. But for most of us happiness is very much influenced by our lifestyle.

In the traditional texts some of the things we will be considering in this chapter are never mentioned. Things like ethics and precepts yes, of course, but lifestyle not really. It is understandable that the Buddha didn't address these things because in his days either they didn't exist, or they weren't problematic. There was no need to seek organic food–all food was organic; there was no need to avoid chemicals; or radiation from electronic devices; there was no issue with water being pure, or air being clean. Most of the things we have to put up with were unknown.

The fact that we grew accustomed to them doesn't make them wholesome. If we add to them the countless demands of modern life, we realise that the whole context of our lives doesn't favour calm and quiet thoughts. We spend the day running around, doing a hundred things and planning a thousand more, pressured by professional demands, family life and interactions with friends. Social networks, text messages, emails and calls at all hours of the day–and night–demand a response and attention, causing wear and tear that we do not always realise. We deal with a huge amount of information, which multiplies the likelihood of violent and devastating emotions that consume what energy we have left. If we add to this the deterioration in the quality of food, air and water and the inherent evils of a sedentary lifestyle and stress, we realise that our habits do not often really meet the conditions for happiness and well-being.

How to get started

Do you spend a lot of time ruminating on negative thoughts, projecting horror films and getting distressed for no reason? When someone doesn't call at the usual time, do you think they've had an accident, been mugged or are ill, even though it's much more likely that they've forgotten, are busy or have no battery left on their mobile phone? Much of the suffering and unease we feel in everyday life comes not from real situations but from our fears and speculations. You've probably realised that the mind can be its own worst enemy, but perhaps you find it difficult to calm mental turbulence and create new trails of thought.

It's important to realise that everything works based on causes and circumstances. For example, a seed has the potential to germinate and become a plant, but only under certain conditions: being in the soil, having humidity, heat and sunlight. The plant it becomes is the result of the interaction between the substantial cause - the seed—and the surrounding circumstances—light, heat, humidity. Everything works in a similar way.

Ignorance of this dynamic leads us to want to change something in isolation from its context. No wonder it doesn't work, everything is largely the result of the surrounding circumstances, and in order to change the result, we have to change the circumstances. That's why lifestyle, nutrition, health and ethics are so important in this process. As in the example of the seed, if we don't meet the conditions for well-being, it will be very difficult to alter the outcome. On the other hand, it only takes a small change for the end result to change. That's why it's possible to improve radically, one small change at a time.

In any effective transformation there is always a first impulse. Sometimes people talk about a *light bulb moment*, a moment of realisation when everything becomes so perfectly clear that the decision comes without any effort. It's a moment we've all felt at one time or another when making a particular choice. Sometimes that light comes on because we've reached the limit or, as they say, hit rock bottom. We've reached a situation so absurd, so desperate, so extreme, that change becomes essential. It doesn't mean that we are necessarily at death's door, but that we have reached an untenable situation, a dead end.

But the light bulb is just the starter. Then we must attain focus, without losing heart, especially if the process of transformation needed to put our lives back together takes some time. It's impossible to make radical changes overnight, we can start with something that, even if it's just a small detail, will improve some area of our life. We must start wherever we can, with as much focus as we can manage, changing whatever is possible. In this way, drop by drop, the largest containers are filled.

Lifestyle

In general, the living conditions to which we are subjected daily are unhealthy. We spend long hours in environments with artificial light and air conditioning, in front of computers, multitasking, drinking coffee and working under pressure. Even when we can relax and be aware of the present moment, we dive into our Smartphone or tablet and again get lost in messages and social media.

If we live in the city, we end up breathing polluted air, eating junk food, drinking sugary drinks and doing very little physical exercise. We spend hours in traffic jams breathing in exhaust fumes and, when we get home, we flop down on the sofa to watch TV. I'm convinced that if one of our tribal ancestors spent a day with us, he'd run away in terror.

The arguments we give ourselves for submitting to this lifestyle and strenuous work are usually material. Many of us have heavy financial obligations and feel they are an impediment to change. Of course, when we have a family to support, children to educate and other commitments, we honour our responsibilities. We can't just quit our jobs. But that doesn't stop us from trying to improve what we can. Sometimes, too, when we analyse our situation honestly, we come to the conclusion that our impediments are not really financial. They might have to do with attachment to a social status or the desire to be recognised by our peers or family, for example, something that has nothing to do with money. Wanting to always have the latest gadget or model of iPhone, feeling compelled to buy the best car or wear expensive shoes may keep us under financial pressure unnecessarily. In order to be able to live a more relaxed and fulfilling life, we have to carefully evaluate our priorities, understanding that the material aspect cannot be considered more important than health or happiness.

These issues of social status, comfort or self-image are likely to create such resistance that it prevents us from seeing the most obvious solutions. We also often refuse to accept them simply because they need a change of habits or mental representations of ourselves and our lifestyle. However, once we overcome the resistance, we can quickly adapt to the new situation and may even discover some advantages in it.

Food

In today's world, the two big industries that control our health are the food industry and the pharmaceutical industry. They are businesses, so we need to bear in mind that they were not created with our well-being in mind: they exist to make profits, and the more the merrier.

In food terms, a simple rule we can follow is this: the more industrially processed a food is, the less nutrients it has and the less fit it is for human consumption. If we read the fine print on the labels, we'll discover that the simplest products, the ones we buy regularly to feed our family, contain an impressive list of mysterious ingredients whose code names start with the letter E followed by a number. These are all sorts of additives, some of them genuinely unfit for human consumption.

Regardless of whether or not we adhere to any kind of food system, it's important to be picky about the quality of the food we eat. For fruit, vegetables, cereals, meat, fish or vegetable proteins we should choose natural, unprocessed and, if possible, organically grown ingredients. The once prohibitive price of organic products has been falling and we can even find them on the shelves of large supermarkets at a price only slightly higher than others. Food from organic farming not only tastes better, it is also free from pesticide residues, fertilisers and other poisons.

Curiously, many people don't hesitate to go on holiday to an exotic destination but don't think it's worth spending a little more on organic products. If we realise that our health depends largely on the quality of what we eat, we might be more willing to review our priorities.

It's commonly thought that Buddhists are necessarily vegetarians, but this is not the case. In Buddhist countries where there was a cultural tradition of vegetarianism, like in India or Thailand, for instance, vegetarianism was the rule for Buddhist monks. However, in Tibet, most lamas and monks, as well as lay practitioners, used to eat meat. It's important to note that Buddhism doesn't forbid or enforce anything. There is a passage in the Lankavattara Sutra where the Buddha clearly states all the negatives aspects of eating meat—but he doesn't forbid it. Like in regard to all other aspects of ethics, it is up to us to decide what makes more sense, considering our situation and our specific needs.

Our ancestors weren't necessarily vegetarians, but they consumed far fewer animal products than we do. The change in eating habits over the last few decades has led to the large-scale rearing of animals for consumption with its consequent horrors. Most people don't know, or prefer to ignore, how animals are raised and slaughtered, what they eat, the antibiotics and hormones they are given and the absolutely inhumane way they are treated. Films such as *Food, Inc., Origins, Forks over Knives, Food Matters* portray the American reality, which is certainly not very different from many Western countries and leave us horrified.

There is unarguably some hypocrisy in the way we mindlessly eat animals. Should we have to kill them ourselves, we would probably have turned vegetarian ages ago. It's common for people to say they can't eat rabbit because they had a rabbit as pet when they were growing up, or they haven't been able eat meat since they watched Bambi. The idea of eating our pets is revolting because for us they are *people* not eatables. The moment we fully recognise animals as sentient beings, it becomes very difficult to eat them, and rightly so. Especially for those following the Mahayana path, it certainly makes sense to avoid meat consumption.

This being said, whatever our choice is, I think it is important to respect other people's choices. However passionate we are about something, that should not give us a reason to judge or condemn anyone.

Health

The food industry controls one part of our lives; the pharmaceutical industry manipulates another. They complement each other perfectly, but they don't have our well-being in mind. Above all, they are businesses and some of the most successful in the world: they make astronomical profits every year.

In the business world, it's very important to build customer loyalty, satisfied customers come back. When it comes to medicines, the satisfied customer is cured–and doesn't come back. That's why the pharmaceutical industry's interest is not in having satisfied customers, people in good health, but chronic patients, loyal consumers, dependant customers.

In general, allopathic medicines are designed to make symptoms disappear–as quickly as possible–and not to treat them. What's more, when we read the list of contraindications and side effects of the most common medicines, we get the feeling that we're taking a poison that our body can only tolerate at a certain dose. Of course, we are trained not to question ourselves and when we feel ill, we are frightened and willing to do anything to end the pain or discomfort. But if we think about it, we might come to the conclusion that it isn't normal for a drug to be so harmful.

By way of comparison, think that in ancient China the doctor was hired to keep the patient in good health and, if he fell ill, he treated him free of charge. The inversion of these values completely perverted the profession and allowed the development of the pharmaceutical industry with its strange conception of what constitutes a medicine. Illness has almost become the norm and health the exception. I don't think this is the way it is supposed to be.

Of course, conventional medicine has made enormous progress, especially in surgery and technological means of diagnosis and can now intervene in borderline situations that a few years ago caused death. However, conventional medicine's approach is to control symptoms and its intervention in the disease process is later than traditional or natural medicine.

These medicines are much more preventative and are focused on maintaining and restoring health. The means of diagnosis are subtle and make it possible to detect an energy imbalance before it becomes physiological and when it can still be easily corrected. If the diet and lifestyle are healthy and natural, the body has all the necessary defence and repair mechanisms. That's why it is essential to strengthen our immune system and be more careful about excessive and unnecessary intake of synthetic medicines.

There are many more preventative medicines we can try: traditional ones such as Chinese, Tibetan or Ayurvedic medicine; but also more recent ones such as homeopathy and integrative medicine. Understandably we may feel unwilling to take these medicines as they are not offered by the medical profession, and may not fall under your health insurance, so are not accessible to the vast majority of people. That's true. That's why it is so important to lead a healthy lifestyle. This way we can prevent a large number of illnesses and feel better on a daily basis.

Habits

If we want to feel better and be happier it's important to eliminate habits that are detrimental to health and physical or mental balance. Excesses of alcohol, tobacco, coffee or sugar overload the body, create dependency and cause physical and mental imbalances. Some people would rather lose years off their lives than give up alcohol or tobacco. They say that if they do, they will deprive themselves of the few pleasures they have left. But if they could learn to relax and open themselves up to new experiences, they would possibly discover other small pleasures that are much more satisfying and have no downsides.

No one today is unaware of the harmful effects of smoking and the fact that in many countries smoking has been banned in public spaces and on public transport is a great achievement for both non-smokers and smokers. The mentality has changed so much that a Belgian anti-smoking campaign used the slogan: "Smoking has gone out of fashion".

Giving up smoking–or any detrimental habit, for that matter–isn't necessarily difficult, as long as we're really determined. Even if we haven't yet reached the necessary level of determination, it is possible to work on it. Thinking about all the disadvantages of smoking will increase a sense of aversion and listing all the advantages of not smoking will make the idea more attractive.

From the point of view of Buddhist teachings, tobacco has a harmful effect on the body's subtle energies. There are energy circuits in our bodies, similar to the meridians in acupuncture, but with a more subtle character. These channels, and the spiritual energy that circulates in them, are responsible for the degree of spirituality and openness to the metaphysical aspects of the world. According to Buddhist teachings, tobacco smoke blocks and clogs these subtle channels, keeping us trapped in a limited and materialistic view of the world. One of the great Tibetan teachers, Dudjom Rinpoche who died in the 1980s, wrote a short text on the harmful effects of tobacco that you can read to learn more about this aspect of the issue[6].

Drinking a glass of wine while enjoying a good meal with friends is obviously not a problem. But if we feel we are drinking too much, it's important to take action. Regular alcohol consumption creates a propensity for emotional imbalance, impairs judgement and diminishes the ability to be attentive. The chemicals in beer can produce negative thinking and lead to depression.

Too much coffee makes us much more irritable and aggressive, unable to control ourselves. It also increases anxiety and restlessness, both physically and mentally. The same can be said of all excitants, such as black tea in large quantities and even cocoa.

We should also be careful with sugar: it has been proven to be responsible for numerous diseases, including obesity and type 2 diabetes, which kill hundreds of thousands of people every year. We are constantly exposed to it not only in sweet desserts, but in

---

[6] "The Harmful Effects of Tobacco", Padmakara Editions.

countless industrially processed foods and drinks, even the most unexpected ones. So even if we don't like sweets and don't drink soft drinks, we're not free from consuming sugar.

Physical exercise and sleep

Sport and physical exercise are fundamental. Our ancestors didn't have this concern because the daily tasks necessary for survival essentially involved movement and physical effort. Modern lifestyle tends to be sedentary. I believe that many of the mental problems, insomnia, anxiety and depression that are so common in our world have a lot to do with a lack of physical exercise. By releasing them physically, tensions and conflicts are minimised and torment us much less. After a physically active day, we sleep well and feel relaxed more easily.

On the contrary, the nervous exhaustion of a day spent indoors, without air or natural light, in front of a computer screen, in the midst of stress and conflict, or with long hours in traffic queues to get home, causes a perverse tiredness that doesn't make for a good night's sleep. The combination of a diet high in toxins and the lack of physical exercise to release them can cause devastation.

For those who don't like energetic endeavours, yoga is an excellent alternative. The exercises work all parts of the body and balance your energy, while helping to combat stress and maintain flexibility. In yoga you learn to take special care with your breathing and to perform the postures (*asanas*) in synchronisation with it. Tai Chi and Qigong are meditative ways of working the body, which also balance the mind.

One essential factor in a healthy life is good sleep patterns. Sleep disorders are responsible for a large proportion of depression. Many people don't get enough sleep, and it's not always because they can't. It often happens that we don't want to give up a few moments to ourselves at the end of the day and we go to bed later than we should. Getting enough sleep is fundamental.

In addition, it's not enough to pay attention to the number of hours of sleep; we have to ensure its quality. It is recommended to set up the bedroom in a less noisy part of the house, away from the front door, and draw the blinds or curtains so that we sleep in darkness. In general, it is preferable to exclude from the bedroom all electronic devices that emit radiation. During sleep, the body and particularly the brain are at rest, and even more permeable to all radiation than in active mode.

If you can, do a few minutes of meditation before you go to sleep. If you wake up during the night, instead of lying in bed brooding over your thoughts, sit down for a few minutes and meditate. You'll find it easier to fall back asleep and, in the event that you don't, at least you'll have used your time for something useful.

Creating a harmonious space

The space where we live and work also has an influence on how we feel. In ancient China, Feng Shui (literally Wind and Water) was used to harmonise and direct the energies present in homes in order to create a favourable environment. Some people are more sensitive to environments than others, but we are all influenced by them.

Certain places are so imbued with energy that even the most insensitive people realise it. Prisons, hospitals and other places where there is a lot of suffering have a heavy, awkward atmosphere that is easy to sense. More commonly, there are houses with a very pleasant atmosphere, where we feel good, and others where the opposite is true. If we're attentive, we may notice that after moving house, some things change in our life, sometimes radically.

Feng Shui has become fashionable over the last few years and countless books on the subject have appeared on the market. Without going into details, there are two fundamental things that are perfectly within our reach and that will make a big difference: order and cleanliness. In a house that is in disarray, dirty and mistreated, with broken or dilapidated appliances and objects, nothing can function properly, and our mind loses clarity and dynamism. We shouldn't keep household appliances or other devices that no longer work, we should have them repaired or throw them away.

If you've ever had to clear out a house, you've probably realised how absurd it is to accumulate so much stuff. We spend time and energy obtaining, organising, storing and keeping things that we rarely use, and we leave it to others to deal with them when we no longer want them or when we die. What a colossal waste of time!

If we are feeling we need a change in our life, we could try to do a big clean-out of our home, starting with a drawer, a cupboard or a room. Karen Kingstone's books[7] on Feng Shui are very practical and inspiring. It is important to surround ourselves with the comfort we

---

[7] Clear your Clutter with Feng Shui and Creating Sacred Space with Feng Shui

need to feel at home and relaxed. Preparing an area of our home to become the place where we meditate can be an important step to achieve a regular practice.

Ethics

After taking care of our lifestyle, we must pay more attention to our attitudes, realising that if we want to transform ourselves in a positive way, we must have ethical principles. In the modern world, it's not very popular to talk about ethics. Our society believes that it's more important to have freedom than ethics, and that any set of rules by which we are supposed to conduct ourselves only interferes and gets in the way.

This might even make sense if we've lost sight of why they exist and think they're just a set of random, unfounded rules that are maintained by habit alone. However, if we realise that all the suffering we cause others has repercussions for us, it's very easy to establish a direct link between ethics and well-being and happiness. The Buddha proposed a very concrete and simple form of ethical behaviour. To each new follower he proposed the adoption of a few principles that are still proposed today: the five precepts.

According to this tradition, a precept is a commitment we make to ourselves, with the Buddha as our witness. The five initial vows are: not to kill, not to steal, not to lie, to have correct sexual behaviour and not to take intoxicants. The various Buddhist traditions have different formulations for these precepts, but their essence is identical.

In the Tibetan tradition, the lama confers the five precepts during a simple ceremony, held in a group, in which each person commits themselves to one, two, three or more of these vows. There is no order. Even if you don't immediately have the opportunity to take part in such a ceremony, you can make the decision to adopt one or more of these precepts. While for some it may not make any sense, at least not immediately, for others the effect can be transformative. Adopting one of these principles and sticking to it at all costs could be exactly the incentive we need to reorganise and give structure to life and improve our self-esteem.

I spoke above about the importance our society places on the freedom to realise our plans, ideas or mere whims. This freedom, however, when exercised without discernment, has led us much more often to chaos and suffering than to harmony and well-being. For a society to function, it is essential that everyone's freedom ends where everyone else's freedom begins.

When we are aware of the effect of interdependence, refraining from doing something that conflicts with our ethics conveys a feeling of freedom and nobility that strengthens and dignifies us. It's important to note that this renunciation must be based on constructive and healthy motives and not a form of self-punishment. The rules of this type of ethics are respected because they make sense and because their positive effects can be seen. The decision to respect them is freely made and is based on an understanding of their raison d'être. Unlike value systems based on fear and punishment from a superior entity, this type of ethics favours personal responsibility and decision-making, generating a very healthy feeling of empowerment.

Do not kill

The first precept is not to kill. In Tibetan Buddhism, this means taking the life of a human being or a human being *in the making* - an embryo. Respect for life–and not just human life–has always been present in the Buddha's teachings. In Tibetan, the word for beings, *semtchen,* means endowed with consciousness and indicates that this is the criterion for distinguishing living beings from others. Conscious beings feel pain and have an instinct for survival, so killing one of them inevitably causes suffering. Although this is easier to recognise in animals that are biologically close to us, this doesn't mean that, in their own way and on their own scale, even the simplest animals don't feel some form of pain.

If this first precept only mentions human beings, it's because the Buddha wanted it to be accessible to both secular and religious people. In his time, most families, especially the poorest, could not survive without killing any animal. However, as said before, Buddha has pointed out that eating meat should be avoided if we try to follow the way of the Mahayana.

If the first part of the precept–not to kill human beings–is agreed upon, the second–not to kill unborn human beings–is much less so. From the point of view of Buddhist teachings, consciousness is present from the moment of conception, so the voluntary termination of pregnancy amounts to killing, which is contrary to this precept. This is a controversial point and, please remember, that it's not a law or a condemnation but something we accept if we understand the reasons behind it. Obviously, there are many different situations and ultimately the point is for us to acknowledge that killing is an action with a negative impact. Some situations are such that there is no good or bad solution, and we will have to go for the least negative one.

Although the first precept does not include animal life forms, avoiding acts of killing in any form is an excellent principle and, therefore, when we formulate our commitment to this precept we can choose the exact terms.

We may ask why we should formalise, by the use of a commitment, a behaviour that is already natural in us. The texts explain that there is a special power in making a commitment and that the positive impact of actions is greater. The main reason for this is that, as soon as there is commitment, there is intention, and it is this that imparts a special power to our actions.

Do not steal

In Tibetan, the word used for this precept literally means *taking what has not been given*. Perhaps it seems obvious and you consider yourself an honest person, but if you take a closer look at your behaviour, you may come to the conclusion that you need to change a few things.

Taking home paperclips, rubber bands or sheets of paper from the office, for example, may seem unimportant or even justified– "after all, they buy in large quantities and it's much cheaper for them" or "so much just gets wasted"–but, in reality, it's an act that goes against this precept. Perhaps you think it's being a bit fundamentalist, especially if you have this habit and see nothing wrong with it. But it's not a question of moral judgement or of being a bit fundamentalist. The idea is not to be politically correct, perfect citizens, obedient and orderly. Nor is it a question of agreeing or disagreeing with the principle of property, but of recognising that we all clearly distinguish between what is ours and what is not. So not respecting this principle exposes us to totally unnecessary hassle and problems, especially if we're talking about ballpoint pens and toilet paper.

The benefits of having an attitude of integrity—even if it's something completely out of fashion—are far greater. In practice, respecting these precepts gives us a feeling of honour and an inner strength that are like the backbone of our mental attitude. Perhaps no one will know that we bring home packets of sugar; perhaps no one will notice and they won't be missed: this attitude, however, erodes our dignity, weakens us and jeopardises our chances of happiness.

Do not lie

This precept inspires us to be true to ourselves, to our abilities, faults and qualities, and to be honest and sincere in what we pass on to others. There are of course many types of lies, some more serious than others. Whenever we lie, we generally hope to reap some benefit, often to the detriment of other people. Serious lies include any type of dishonesty that make people trust us in a spiritual, emotional, or material way so we can take advantage of them, and obviously, lies told with the real intention of harming.

Whenever we talk about lying, questions arise about so-called white lies, i.e. lies whose purpose is to spare others suffering. For the intention to be truly positive we must have nothing to gain from it and the information we pass on must not harm anyone.

Whatever the purpose of a lie, it always generates a certain amount of tension. Even a white lie can force us to pay close attention so as not to betray ourselves, to tell more lies to cover up the first one and to force other people to lie as well.

It is interesting to note that being honest and telling the truth can bring us many advantages, even in material terms. In India, the followers of Jainism have the reputation of being honest. They were mostly businessmen and follow several ethic vows, including those of truthfulness, not stealing and non-greediness. As businessmen they were the most trusted and thus the most successful. They are the richest religious community in India, with more than 70% of their population in the top quintile.

Moreover, if we behave honestly, we are promoting honesty and conversely, if we behave dishonestly, we are fostering dishonesty. If someone is honest with us, we will be more inclined to be honest with them than if that person is deceitful, won't we? As human beings we tend to copy others and adopt their standards, so when we see dishonesty, we feel justified to act in the same way.

Sometimes we may wonder how we can make this world a better place: by acting in a positive and virtuous way, no matter how difficult or old fashioned it might look. Even in small and apparently non-important things we can set an example for others and create the causes for being able to be relaxed and confident, with a clear conscience.

Correct sexual behaviour

Obviously, incorrect sexual behaviour like engaging in sexual activities by force, with inappropriate or unwilling partners or other such devious behaviours are a given. Therefore, essentially this precept means that we commit ourselves not to have sexual relations with anyone committed to someone else or with anyone other than our partner. This precept doesn't need a long explanation: we all know the devastating effects of this type of situation.

If you've ever been involved in a love triangle, you know from experience that no one escapes unscathed. Because they trigger some of the most powerful and overwhelming negative emotions, these situations often reveal what is most destructive in human beings.

Normally people see precepts as something that restricts freedom and, therefore, particularly nowadays, as something that prevents them from being happy. In reality, precepts are a protection against the devastating emotions that cloud our judgement and lead us to commit acts that we bitterly regret. In this particular case, there are many people who have never imagined cheating on their partners until they find themselves in a situation where, under the influence of emotions they can't control, they lose their judgement completely. The results are often devastating for everyone involved, directly or indirectly, and the benefit is almost non-existent.

The great merit of this precept is that it creates an extra barrier of restraint, a waiting period that allows us to act without rushing into things. If we are firmly convinced of the power and raison d'être of these precepts, we will hesitate to break them out of hand.

TSERING PALDRON

Do not take intoxicants

The fifth precept refers to not ingesting substances that can cloud our clarity of mind: alcohol, drugs or any natural or synthetic substances that make us lose our state of presence. This precept may seem strange and much less essential than killing or stealing, for example. The anecdote that is told about it helps us to better understand why it exists.

It is said that a Buddhist monk was once taken prisoner by non-Buddhist villains who had a bet on how they would make him break his vows. They locked him in a cell with a woman, a goat and a jug of wine and told him they would kill him unless he had sex with the woman, killed the goat or drank the wine. After much thought, the monk thought that of the three negative acts, the least serious was drinking the wine. So he did. However, when he woke up the next day, he realised that, under the influence of alcohol, he had killed the goat and had sex with the woman.

It's also important to understand the context of this vow. In the East, there was no custom of drinking wine or beer to accompany a meal. In general, in Eastern countries, when you drink alcohol, it's always to excess. In this cultural context, the need for this precept becomes clearer.

The problem with abusing these substances is that they make us lose our clarity of mind and, along with it, our sense of reality and limits. And the danger is significantly higher for those who normally hold a greater degree of restraint. Societies or people under great pressure and with very strict rules are also often those in which alcohol abuse has the most disastrous effects.

Of course, we can take this precept to the letter and not touch alcohol at all, or we can maintain social consumption so that we don't distance ourselves from our friends and can socialise healthily. In this case, as in all others, we decide the exact terms of our commitment, taking into account what we consider to be balanced and harmonious.

Ethics are a personal matter

Buddhism is a method of personal transformation in which each individual takes responsibility for their own training. Thus, these precepts (or any others, including the monastic vows themselves) are a personal matter that doesn't concern anyone else.

No one checks whether or not we are fulfilling what we've promised, and no one comes to punish us if we are not respecting our vows. When we commit to these principles, we are supposed to understand their raison d'être and be convinced that they are relevant and useful. It is also essential that it makes sense for us to adopt them as ethical principles of life. Therefore, if we betray them, we betray ourselves.

If you want to commit to one or more of these principles, start by choosing the one or ones that seem most important to you, that are easiest or, on the contrary and depending on the goal you want to achieve, the one or ones that are most necessary. Doing so in the presence of a spiritual teacher or instructor, in a place you consider sacred or inspiring, in a temple or in front of a statue of Buddha will be a way to reinforce the intention and make that moment and that commitment anything but trivial. You could, for example, put it in writing and sign it, so that this moment is recorded as something important, sealed with the determination to do what you can not to break the commitment you have made.

Some people take these issues very lightly and believe that commitments are made to be broken. Others take everything very seriously, with great intransigence towards themselves and others. While the former often don't want to take vows or do so in a very non-committal way, the latter hesitate to do so for fear of not being able to keep them.

If we don't have a clear idea of the importance of a vow and don't feel a persistent determination to respect it, it's perfectly pointless to take it. The idea is that it should help us to change our behaviour and give us a sense of dignity and righteousness, which are the foundations of a happier and more fulfilled life.

But if it makes sense to us, we should realise what the right attitude is towards this decision. As I've already said, we must be perfectly determined to honour our commitments, whatever the cost, and if, for some reason beyond our control, we can't do it, we have to be ready to take responsibility. It's better to commit to just one of these life principles and respect it than to commit to all and respect none of them.

On the other hand, if we happen to break our promises, we need to do something to restore our inner attitude. It's not a question of confessing in front of someone who will pat us on the shoulder and say that everything is fine. Unfortunately, restoring inner dignity is much more demanding than that. We must recognise that we were carried away by our emotions or simply inattentive, feel deep regret, do something to make amends and make the decision not to break our promises again.

We should be careful because our most destructive tendencies may seize the opportunity to discourage us from everything, in a *miss by an inch, miss by a mile* reaction. There's no point in fuelling guilt or beating ourselves up about what happened. We should just let go and start again.

If you have accumulated too many transgressions, it can be difficult to regain your initial enthusiasm. It's better to forget the whole process, but not just anyhow. In order to be consistent and somehow not lose respect for yourself, it is important to revoke the vows, that is, deliberately and under the same conditions as before, state that you no longer wish to, or cannot, maintain that life ethic. Ideally, you should do this before you have broken them, so that the energy of self-respect is not lost.

To avoid the weakening caused by not keeping our commitments, we can decide at the outset how long we want to keep them for: a month, six months, a year... Then, if everything goes well, we can renew the period. If it's something we find difficult to keep, knowing that it's only for a certain period can help us get the most out of it without any contraindications.

Finally, keep in mind that the idea behind all these methods is to help us build a healthier and more harmonious life, a sense of integrity and honesty as the backbone of our inner attitude, and not to provide us with yet another way of torturing ourselves. Buddhism has a number of methods adapted to the different capacities and aptitudes of beings and we don't have to practise them all. We should adopt the ones that make sense and are effective for us at the moment and make the most of them to build and harmonise ourselves.

Practical tips from chapter 2:

- Be careful with the foods you eat, choose foods that are as close to their natural state as possible and avoid anything that is industrially processed.
- When it comes to your health, take a preventative medicine approach and look after your immune system.
- Give up harmful habits with strategy and wisdom.
- Exercise and create the conditions for a good rest.
- Create a harmonious space in your home and get rid of everything you don't use.
- Adopt one or more ethical precepts and respect them

• CHAPTER 3 •

LIVING FROM THE HEART

Much of the happiness and suffering we experience depends on the relationships we have with others. It's not possible to be fully happy alone, independent from our surroundings, nor can we do it if we're entangled in conflicts or disputes of any kind. That's why it's so important to develop qualities of heart.

Tibetan teachers often say that the essence of Buddhist practice is to cultivate a good heart. For some of us the idea that it's possible to become more warm-hearted might seem strange. We are convinced that one is born more or less empathetic, that emotions cannot be worked through by reason and that there is an intrinsic conflict between the heart and the head.

Our culture has been very focused on logical and rational intelligence and has valued it to the extreme. For decades, IQ was used as a measure of individuals' cognitive ability and a generalised prejudice attributed a high IQ to a mark of superiority. However, people with very high IQs sometimes show a great inability to manage emotions, empathise and interact harmoniously with others.

In recent decades we have started to talk about another type of intelligence: Emotional Intelligence (EQ), which is characterised as the ability to recognise emotions, understand their meaning and manage them well in interactions with others. More recently, a third type of intelligence has been accepted: spiritual intelligence (SQ), which has to do with the meaning we attach to life and the values that regulate our behaviour.

The ability to be happy depends much more on the last two types of intelligence than on the first. Many centuries before all these discoveries, Buddha taught how to harmonise all these types of intelligence so that we can live a balanced life.

Interdependent origination

The Buddhist method doesn't suggest that we abandon reason. On the contrary, we are supposed to use it to reflect for ourselves, with an open mind, and analyse reality. We often don't realise how we've been shaped by culture, society, and education. We express, with the conviction that they are ours, beliefs and opinions that we have received and have never questioned. On the other hand, we're also not aware of how they influence our view of the world and how this, in turn, conditions our experience. I therefore suggest that we reflect on an essential point of Buddhist philosophy: interdependent origination.

In a very empirical way and even without realising it, we all believe that the world is made up of phenomena and people, solid, existing and independent of each other. If true, this means that any object has its own inherent qualities such as colour, shape, weight, etc. which remain unchanged whatever the context. When we look at an object and see blue, we assume that it is intrinsically blue and that its colour remains the same in any situation. However, we know that the colour depends on how the light falls and how the surface of the object reflects it. In practice, it depends on the time of day, the positioning of the object in relation to the light source, etc. Thus, it is only blue at certain times and under a certain type of lighting.

Let's examine other characteristics. Weight depends on the force of gravity to which the object is exposed, and this depends on its mass. On Earth, on the Moon, on Mars or outside any gravitational field, the same object has different weights. The shape can depend on factors such as pressure or temperature. And so on. This simple analysis allows us to conclude that none of its characteristics are fixed, unalterable and definite, that they all depend on the conditions and context in which the object finds itself.

This becomes even more evident when we ask ourselves questions like: What colour, shape or weight does an object have outside of any context? Without a light source, without the force of gravity, without a defined temperature or pressure, what would that object be like? There is no answer to this and therefore the conclusion seems to be that objects do not have their own inherent characteristics and do not exist on their own. Their characteristics only exist as causal interactions with other phenomena. Buddha called this interdependent origination.

If everything is so structurally interconnected that nothing can exist on its own, outside of any context, the feeling that we are separate from others and from all phenomena is an illusion. In this way, everything we do, say and think changes the things and people around us, and everything around changes us. What we are and feel at every moment is an interaction with our surroundings and, therefore, for us to feel good, it is essential that these interactions are harmonious, both with beings and with the environment.

As an example, we now know that a great percentage of all the cells in the human body are not human but bacteria, fungi and other microorganisms. We are an ecosystem and Paul Hawken, an environmentalist, journalist and author, says this: "The first living cell came into being nearly 40 million centuries ago, and its direct descendants are in all of our bloodstreams. Literally you are breathing molecules this very second that were inhaled by Moses, Mother Teresa, and Bono. We are vastly interconnected. Our fates are inseparable. We are here because the dream of every cell is to become two cells. In each of you are one quadrillion cells, 90 percent of which are not human cells. Your body is a community, and without those other microorganisms you would perish in hours. Each human cell has 400 billion molecules conducting millions of processes between trillions of atoms. The total cellular activity in one human body is staggering: one septillion actions at any one moment, a one with twenty-four zeros after it. In a millisecond, our body has undergone ten times more processes than there are stars in the universe–exactly what Charles Darwin foretold when he said science would discover that each living creature was a little universe, formed of a host of self-propagating organisms, inconceivably minute and as numerous as the stars of heaven!"

I think this example amply demonstrates the reality of interdependence applied to our own physical existence. Understanding phenomena through interdependence means understanding that we are not watertight entities, independent of our surroundings, but rather the convergence and interaction of an immense number of factors. That what we eat, breathe, think and sense have a decisive influence on how we feel and even how we perceive the world.

When we use reason intelligently, we realise that negative attitudes and the actions that result from them are a source of unhappiness and that, conversely, positive states and the actions that result from them are a source of well-being. We are so structurally linked to others that they are a natural extension of ourselves and harming them is as absurd as a hand hurting an arm. When this understanding becomes part of our way of seeing the world, we no longer feel separate, different and isolated from each other. This new awareness enables a balanced and healthy opening of the heart that is not caused by an emotional state but is based on something real.

Cultivating altruism

In general, most of us value altruism but we don't think we can apply it in our everyday lives. When we think of altruism, we imagine Mother Teresa or the Dalai Lama and, as much as we admire them, it's not certain that we want to copy them. That's why, although we value altruism, we never think that putting the care of others before self is a practical way of living.

If we have this warped idea of altruism, it's because we see the world in a dualistic way: it's us against the rest, us or others, and our interests are difficult to reconcile. We think we must favour our own interests, or we'll lose out. Consequently, altruism is synonymous with selflessness and sacrifice, with giving up our will or our interests in favour of others. That's why, although it's morally valued, altruism isn't very appealing. However, if separation is an illusion and we are totally interdependent, when we do good for others, we also gain from it. Our well-being and that of others are not only reconcilable, they are inseparable!

One of the most frequent statements in Buddhism is that all beings desire happiness. Of course, the concept of happiness is very subjective, and some may even have a perverted notion of it. However, from the moment we get up until we go to bed, and even in our dreams, everything we do, say and think is aimed at obtaining pleasure and satisfaction, while avoiding suffering and pain. In this respect we are all the same. Races, colours, social strata and cultures may determine what we consider to be happiness and suffering, but they don't differentiate us in our desire to achieve well-being and avoid pain. Therefore, there is no objective reason why some should have more right to fulfil their desire than others. It is not legitimate to think that I, or anyone else, has a greater right to happiness and there is no argument that could validate such a thought.

The reality is simple: would we accept that someone else's interests were more important than ours? On the other hand, unless they are completely self-centred, anyone can accept that their interests are put on an equal footing with those of another person. On that basis, we can realise that neither do others have to lower themselves before us, nor do we have to erase ourselves before them. The basis of Buddhist altruism is this objective and egalitarian perspective, which respects the good of all. Therefore, in all of life's decisions, for our own good, it is advisable to opt for what best preserves everyone's interests.

Because of the idea we have of altruism as the denial of our interests, we have the impression that, although politically correct, positive and admirable, it is only optional. Many of us consider altruism to be an attitude of goodwill, appropriate for beings devoid of material ambition, orientated towards the good of others, but counterproductive for ordinary beings who, in everyday life, must earn a living, educate their children, pay the bills, etc.

The Buddhist altruistic attitude is essentially that of a broadening of vision. Instead of thinking of me, we think of all of us: "I want to be happy and I don't want to suffer" becomes "We all want to be happy and we don't want to suffer"; or "I want to be treated well" becomes "We all want to be treated well"; or "I want my interests to be respected" becomes "We all want our interests to be respected", etc. We don't always realise that this attitude simplifies our lives rather than complicating them. Because it's realistic and pragmatic, it makes our lives easier and much less contrary. It may seem paradoxical, but altruism is first and foremost good for us. The fact that we wish all beings happiness, in itself, doesn't bring them any benefit, but it makes us feel much better.

Many people think that this is an impossible attitude in today's world and that, if you're a good person, there will immediately be people who take advantage of you. It's understandable. But altruism doesn't have to make us easy prey for malicious people. This attitude is not necessarily naive. Wishing others well is not incompatible with discernment, common sense, and lucidity. Empathising with human beings doesn't stop us from being prudent or demanding that they treat us fairly and with respect. The difference is in the way and the reasons why we do it.

To avoid suffering, we have to renounce actions that cause suffering to others because it inevitably has repercussions on us. This is fundamental, but it's not enough to make us happy. To do this, we need to cultivate a positive intention, a warm disposition and a good heart. When we wish others well, offering kindness and compassion, we are the first to benefit from these feelings. That's why His Holiness the Dalai Lama says: "The short-sighted egoist is simply selfish. But the intelligent egoist is altruistic."

Cultivating a positive predisposition

Even without realising it, your predisposition towards others may not be positive. In general, people's predominant feeling towards strangers is one of almost hostile indifference. This feeling is by no means a source of happiness and well-being and it's important to cultivate a warmer attitude and a feeling of closeness that makes us feel sympathetic rather than hostile.

We all want to be happy, and we all find this desire to be legitimate, so no one likes when it isn't respected. The problem is that when we put our interests above those of others, we put ourselves in a position of potential conflict, since this overvaluation clashes with the aspiration of others for well-being. This implicit conflict gives rise to deep-seated hostility and the notion that other people's interests threaten our happiness. We need to change this perspective.

The presence of others in the world is not a source of unhappiness, quite the opposite. Throughout our lives, there have been many people who have helped us, cared for us and whose existence has marked us in a profoundly positive way. Let's start with our parents. Even if they weren't exemplary, they brought us up and educated us, to the best of their ability. As we said, ultimately, they are just human beings, with flaws and defects like the rest of us and, however imperfect they may be, we owe them our lives.

Thanks to teachers we have knowledge that is very useful to us; without the support and affection of family and friends many things in our lives would have been impossible. The number of people who love us, help us or, even without knowing it, make our existence possible and enjoyable is virtually infinite. There is no service or object that does not depend on the labour or goodwill of others. We mustn't forget that we only survived as a species because we came together in groups. In isolation, we would have disappeared long ago.

The following exercise might help you make this more concrete. Take a sheet of paper. Think of a particularly happy situation in your life, be it past, present or even imagined. Write down the names of everyone who contributed to it. Don't just think of those directly involved, try to go deeper. For example, if one of the happiest moments in your life was the birth of one of your children, don't just write down your spouse's and your child's names. Think of your parents and ancestors, without whom you wouldn't exist. Think of the doctors, nurses and hospital staff. Think of those who built it, those who made the beds, the appliances, the windows, the doors, the reinforced concrete, the ambulances. Those who make sure there is water, electricity and gas; those who take care of the heating, those who extract the metals, those who grow the cotton for the sheets, those who harvest it, those who spin it, those who weave it. A thousand sheets of paper wouldn't be enough to contain the names of all those who have contributed to the tiniest moment of happiness. We can't be happy without others.

As we can see, we have every reason to be grateful to others and to wish them well. Friends, enemies and strangers all contribute to our happiness and well-being, both in extreme circumstances and in everyday life. In the most critical situations, they are the ones who donate the blood and organs that save our lives and the lives of our dear ones. They are the ones who rescue us from floods and rubble, from earthquakes and typhoons, and they are the ones who extinguish the flames of fire. They are the ones who drive the ambulances, attend to us in the emergency room and treat us when we are ill. At the beginning and end of life, when our dependence is most visible, they are the ones who look after us and support us. The number of times our lives have been in their hands is unlimited.

If we rarely think with gratitude about those to whom we owe our lives, only deeper reflection leads us to think about those who contribute anonymously and invisibly to our comfort and well-being. Those who drive the buses and trains we use every day. Those responsible for water, electricity, gas and telephone supplies. Those who grow, harvest, transport and sell all the food on which our lives depend. Those who work on the oil rigs, those who mine, those who clean the streets and gardens, those who work in the water treatment plants. Those who fish, those who cook, those who manufacture the electronic components of computers, in short, all those without whom the things that make us comfortable and which we often only properly appreciate when we lack them, would not exist. There's nothing we use that hasn't been made possible through the participation, kindness or sacrifice of others. Without them, we couldn't survive and any well-being or happiness would be impossible.

If we have reflected in this way, we will naturally move on to the next stage: feeling grateful for everything that others do for us. Just like our parents, who gave us life, watched over us and brought us up, they have also saved our lives countless times and contribute to our well-being and happiness on a daily basis. The least we can do is wish them the happiness they deserve.

Cultivating empathy

As human beings we have the natural ability to put ourselves in someone else's shoes and imagine what they are feeling, to let ourselves be infected by their emotions. This ability, however, varies from person to person. Potentially, it's present in everyone, but for various reasons it doesn't manifest itself in the same way.

When we are too focused on separation, we emphasise the differences between ourselves and others. In this case, empathy is difficult and we become more impervious to other people's feelings. If this separateness is topped up with some ideology, we can go to the extreme of thinking, for example, that people of a certain race or culture don't deserve to live, aren't worthy of compassion or don't have feelings. We've had the most far-fetched examples of this throughout history, but all starts with the hostile indifference we feel towards strangers, especially if they're a little different from us. We sense this difference as strange and that's why we call people we don't know *strangers*. I can't help but think about how dogs bark furiously at each other when they are at opposed sides of a fence and get along perfectly as soon as the gate is open.

We have much more in common with others than we realise. If we go into the details, we will obviously find many differences, but in what is essential, we are all the same: we all want to be happy and avoid suffering. We all need vital things like food, clothing and shelter; we all want to be loved; we all crave attention, affection and friendship. We all want to protect the people we care about and we all experience joy and pain. Whatever someone's race, colour, social status or appearance, we can be pretty sure that their joy and pain feels the same as ours.

Sometimes at workshops or retreats where we meet new people, it's interesting to note how the initial strangeness gives way to a feeling of empathy. At first, the way people dress, speak or move, the fact that they are pretty or ugly, fat or thin, can generate judgements, social prejudices or even rejection. But once we interact, we discover commonalities, similar ways of feeling and identical experiences, and the reticence of the first impression dissolves. Of course, we might feel closer to some people than others, but we identify, at least in some ways, with everyone.

As this is the first requirement for developing a warmer attitude, if we're not naturally an empathetic person, we'll need to cultivate this human quality. Whenever we meet someone new or are with someone we dislike, we can reflect on the following five points, making sure they aren't just empty phrases. We can consider the person and think:

Like me, this person just wants to be happy.
Like me, this person wants to avoid suffering.
Like me, this person has experienced sadness, loneliness and despair.
Like me, this person is looking to fulfil their needs.
Like me, this person makes mistakes, and sometimes does the right things.

Repeat this exercise as many times as you need to, until you feel how true it is with anyone, no matter who they are. Train yourself wherever you are, at work, with your family, on public transport or even while watching the news. You'll see that after a while, every time you look at someone, you'll feel much closer and more empathetic. If you are having difficulty forgiving someone, I suggest changing the last line into *like this person, I also make mistakes and sometimes do the right things*. Feel how true it is.

Daring to be vulnerable

The great obstacle that stands between us and empathy is the fear of suffering, the fear that if we break down the barriers that separate us from others, life will become unbearable. This is what happens to those who are very exposed to suffering, like health professionals for example, who become desensitised to protect themselves.

Even if we don't have this exposure to other people's suffering, we all go through painful experiences throughout our lives. Depending on how sensitive we are and how often we've been hurt, we tend to protect ourselves by closing off and armouring our hearts. The problem is that these efforts to eliminate discomfort result in indiscriminate numbness. We manage to stop feeling the *bad* but, inevitably, we also stop feeling the *good*. And so we numb ourselves.

Living, cowering in the depths of fear, is sad and counterproductive. The more we close ourselves off and feel alone, different and separate, the more we suffer and the more fragile we become. In order to find happiness, we have to open up. When we realise that we are all in a difficult situation, that we all share the joys and pains of the human condition, fear is replaced by empathy.

If we've spent many years shielded, it can be terrifying to come out into the open. At first, it might be easier to open up to strangers, because we don't fear their judgements or their exposing our weaknesses. Looking after a pet is also an excellent way of giving and receiving affection. It's a good way to start for those who have become hypersensitive to human contact. Although excellent, it doesn't replace human contact–it complements it and can definitely be a good place to start.

Daring to feel vulnerable is accepting that suffering is part of life and, consequently, of our human experience. It's accepting to open up in the knowledge that life is bittersweet and that it's possible we might get hurt, but that this is the risk to take in order to experience the beauty, goodness and wonder of life.

Compassion vs empathy

What allows us to generate the confidence to step out of our protective shell is the development of compassion. Empathy is very natural and it is the basis for compassion, but because suffering–be it ours or others–creates aversion, we will always feel the need to protect ourselves against it. That is why it is crucial to evolve empathy into compassion.

There are several crucial differences between both. The first is that empathy can be paralysing. If we get stuck in empathy, we become overwhelmed by the suffering of others and, feeling unable to do anything about it, we can fall into cogitation, distress and discouragement. People prone to empathetic responses are also more likely to become despondent and depressed. This is particularly critical in situations where we feel powerless, as it is often the case. Then, when we think about all the suffering in the world, we can lose heart and generate an immense disbelief in humanity.

Compassion, on the other hand, is constructive and proactive. We are sensitive to the suffering of others but, instead of feeling *with them*, we feel *for them* and seek ways in which we can help whether directly or indirectly. With compassion, we consciously choose to turn emotion into action.

It is also very important to realise that empathy is impulsive, unlike compassion, which is intentional. Empathy is the automatic reaction that makes us feel the emotions of others with the same degree of intensity and, sometimes, lack of discernment. When we're under the influence of emotions, we can't think clearly, so the feelings, thoughts and decisions we make are mainly unconsciously generated. The decisions we make based on empathy don't weigh up consequences and are often completely disproportionate and ineffective.

Compassion, on the other hand, by distancing itself from pure emotion, is much more reflective and deliberate. The feelings, thoughts and decisions born of compassion pass through the filters of conscience, they are processed by things like values, ethical principles of justice and universality, which means they are wiser, more impartial, and overall much more effective. With compassion, we weigh up the consequences of our actions and look for solutions that minimise negative outcomes and optimise positive ones.

Another difference is that empathy is exhausting, unlike compassion, which is regenerating. When empathy is triggered by the suffering of others, we are bombarded by negative emotions and experiences which, over time, deplete our resources and damage our mental well-being. This is the well-known burn-out so many health professionals, caregivers or volunteers in emergency situations experience when confronted with the suffering of others for long periods of time.

In contrast to empathy, compassion is characterized by feelings of warmth, concern, and care for others, as well as a strong motivation to improve their wellbeing. Instead of withdrawing in self-defence, compassion enables us to be present with the person in need without experiencing distress.

This is the critical property of compassion that differentiates it from empathy. Because compassion generates positive emotions, it counteracts the negative effects of empathy elicited by experiencing others' suffering. Unlike the dopamine depletion that occurs from activation of the pain networks, the neural networks activated when we feel compassion towards others activate brain areas linked to reward processing, making the experience positive and gratifying. Being able to help makes us feel very good. Helping is rewarding and we are motivated to do it again. In this way, compassion does not fatigue — it is neurologically rejuvenating!

Another big difference is that while empathy divides, compassion unifies. Empathy is the tendency to join in the suffering of others, especially those close to us. Driven by empathy, we are capable of great sacrifices and even giving our lives for strangers, as long as they are recognised as belonging to the group. But when it comes to helping those outside the group, we're not so ready. Recent studies have revealed that the empathy triggered by social connection makes it more likely that individuals belonging to an outgroup will be dehumanised. At the extreme, group empathy can fuel aversion to those who are different from us.

Compassion, on the other hand, is sympathy for the suffering of others, regardless of their social or personal identity. It is the perspective that in anyone's suffering there is a common humanity–the recognition that, regardless of someone's culture, race, sexual orientation or age, we are equal in our desire not to suffer and to be happy. Compassion requires us to rise above prejudice and partisanship to see all people as human beings with the same value.

As Buddhists, we should realise that, by being mistaken about the nature of reality, we all accumulate causes of suffering. Therefore, a fundamental aspect of Buddhist compassion is the wish that beings could not only be free from suffering but also avoid creating what causes it, meaning negative actions. Normally, when we witness a situation in which one person is harming another, ordinary compassion may side with the person who is suffering and against the one who is causing suffering.

However, if we believe that creating suffering for others is what causes our own suffering, then today's perpetrator might be tomorrow's victim. Therefore, while the wish that beings are free from suffering applies to those who are suffering, the wish that they avoid the causes of suffering applies to those who are harming others. In other words, there is no one who is not the object of such compassion.

People often wonder if this kind of compassion, which applies to victims and persecutors, doesn't lead to an acceptance of injustice and an inability to react. What should we do with the anger we feel towards such injustice? It's perfectly natural to feel disgust, we shouldn't be indifferent to the injustices and horrors we witness around us. But the question is against what or whom we direct this disgust. In general, we blame the people directly responsible, but a more reflective attitude allows us to place them in their context and realise that they are not the only ones responsible. Everything is the result of a set of causes and circumstances in which the environment or family, society or the political, cultural or economic situation also play an important role. An even deeper reflection directs our revolt against the conflicting emotions and ignorance that lead people to commit or be complicit in such actions.

This perspective doesn't exonerate the people involved, but it allows us to understand that we can't point to them as being solely responsible. By placing them in their context, we realise that many other factors are involved and that, unless and until they learn to be more aware of their actions and less commanded by their automatic patterns, they are equally victims of their own ignorance. True compassion can be born from this realisation.

But should we act when we witness something that we consider to be unjust or cruel? As far as we can, sensibly and with understanding, of course we should. With compassion for both people, we can try to prevent one of them from harming the other. When it comes to taking action, however, it's important to check whether our intention is really to alleviate the suffering of others or just to dispel the discomfort it creates in us: the suffering of others is so intolerable that we are willing to do anything to put an end to it. However, because in that case our motivation is essentially selfish, our behaviour can become obstinate and blind. On the other hand, if our aim is truly to end the other person's suffering, our help will be useful and appropriate. We will do what we can and accept that we may not be able to solve the situation.

People sometimes feel that being a compassionate person is rather depressing. However, Buddhist compassion is very hopeful. Because we know that our true nature is Buddhahood, we understand that suffering is illusory and temporary, like a bad dream. Since the possibility of going beyond all suffering exists, it is not all doom and gloom. However bad the present situation may be, it can and it will improve.

Compassion is an essential part of the Buddhist path. It is often cultivated in conjunction with three other human qualities, love, joy and impartiality. It is the combination of these four that create a balanced and dignified attitude characterising the Buddhist approach to life.

Cultivating selfless love

What is love? When we say we love somebody, the word refers to many different feelings that range from rather liking to passionately wanting. Love can be wonderful, beautiful, and selfless, but also violent and gruesome, possessive, and exclusive. Selfless love is rare.

As human beings we have a natural fondness for love and tenderness which is consistent with the goodness of our Buddha nature. But then, because of not knowing who or what we really are, we also feel insecure and need constant reassurance and stability. These two feelings are opposed in nature for whereas the first is selfless, the second is self-centred. We might call the first love and the second attachment.

For us, samsaric beings, it is nearly impossible to experience love without attachment. When we love someone our sense of security and stability come to depend on that person–someone we might not have met before last week. We tend to see them as the main source of our happiness in such a way that we only desire their well-being insofar it doesn't collide with ours. They can be happy, for as long as they are ours.

This kind of love–attachment–is anything but selfless and that's why it can be so painful and turbulent. The people we say we love the most are the ones we expect the most from and they are also the ones who make us suffer the most when they upset the fragile balance between their well-being and ours, bringing our world crashing down.

The Buddhist example of unconditional love is a mother's love. Supposedly, no matter what the child does, the mother will never stop loving them and her love does not ask for retribution. Even for a mother this isn't easy because there is often all sorts of expectations.

The more dependence there is on the object of our love, the less selfless our love is likely to be and, consequently, the more difficult it will be for it to bring peace and harmony.

In Buddhist training, love is defined as the wish for all beings to have happiness and the causes of happiness. This definition contains two essential elements that are worth emphasising. Firstly, it is a feeling that encompasses ALL beings, or at least as many as possible. The love we know is an exclusive feeling that encompasses a very small number of beings. And the more we focus on them, the more we feel indifferent or even hostile to others. For this reason, the more our well-wishing expands and the more beings it encompasses, the less tormenting it is and the more it brings us and others true happiness and great well-being.

Secondly, we want beings to create the causes for happiness. And what are they? According to the Buddhist view, happiness is the result of positive and wholesome actions and, therefore, we aren't just thinking about immediate well-being but also about long-term happiness and harmony.

Thus, this love is all-encompassing and open, imbued with understanding. We understand the wishes and desires of others, but we also realise that not everything they want is positive or actually contributes to their well-being. This love is infused with wisdom and a sense of responsibility. Not because we feel better informed, more qualified or in any way superior to others, but because we want the best for them. Wanting what is good for all amounts to wishing that everyone finds their own happiness but excludes the possibility of them obtaining it selfishly and inconsiderately. It is a very wise and enveloping love and the fact that it is not exclusive does not in any way diminish its intensity. On the contrary, as our mind becomes more open and warmer, we begin to see all beings as our close relatives. In any case, there are so many of us on this planet who are so interdependent that it's impossible for the discomfort of some not to interfere with the happiness of the others.

This gradually gives rise to a sense of social responsibility, in the way we interact with others, whether in emotional or professional relationships, or as citizens of the world. We become sincerely concerned and involved in matters of general interest, we reflect on the issues of our time and we constantly seek to promote human values, tolerance, understanding and harmony around us.

We often think that one person alone can't do much to change the world, but history shows us that many big changes often began with the thought or initiative of a single person. Furthermore, if we can have a positive effect on 5 people and each of them on another five, and so on and so forth, there can be a ripple effect that actually improves the world. Mother Teresa of Calcutta once said: "We know only too well that what we are doing is nothing more than a drop in the ocean. But if the drop were not there, the ocean would be missing something."

Feeling the joy

There will always be problems in the world and there will always be difficulties in our lives. We spend our days solving problems: how to pay the mortgage; what to make for dinner; how to bring up the children; who to ask to look after the dog or much worse... We can turn it into a drama and think that we'll only be fine when we've sorted everything out. The problem is that this is not likely to happen.

The great teachers of the past in Tibet realised the nature of reality and reduced their needs as much as possible. They spent their retreats in caves, entirely dedicated to spiritual practice, surrounded only by strictly necessary objects. The number of problems they had to solve during the day was minimal: there were no broken pipes, no railway strikes, no need to set up the wifi or restart the printer... The daily meal was *tsampa*[8]–the first 100 per cent natural fast food–so there wasn't much to worry about.

The comforts and facilities of modern city life have inevitably multiplied problems and their resolution. The more objects we own, the more things we must manage and the more stress we have. That's why the first thing we need to do is simplify our lives as much as possible, getting rid of everything that isn't indispensable and we'll immediately have far fewer worries.

In addition, we can accept that life is just like that, no longer defer our happiness and live joyfully in the present moment. Resolve

---

[8] Tsampa is roasted barley flour that Tibetans mix with tea and butter. Depending on the proportions, it can form porridge or a ball.

whatever can be resolved and do what we can to improve things around us, for ourselves and for others. We should realise that for every problem we face, there is an infinite number of things that work and go well. And above all, we shouldn't anticipate! If we have to face something painful tomorrow, we'll have to do it anyway, whether we worry about it today or not. Better deal with tomorrow's problems tomorrow. Someone once said: "The past is past, the future is a mystery, the present is a gift and that's why it's called the present." With this kind of understanding, everything becomes lighter and brighter.

Empathy, compassion and love are not complete if we don't add joy to them. Sometimes we're so wrapped up in dark thoughts that it almost seems impossible to feel joyful. Depending on the person, joy can be harder to cultivate even than compassion or love. However, you may have already experienced, at certain moments in your life a deep joy that lives within you, independent of circumstances. That joy is the nature of our mind! So, if we can free ourselves from the worries that overshadow it, joy will be there, waiting for us.

Until then, we can cultivate this feeling by choosing to think about happy things and spend time with positive people. Emotions are very contagious so, at least in the beginning, it's important to choose who we spend most of our time with. When joy has become a habit, we can be the ones to positively influence others, but until then, it's important to expose ourselves, as much as possible, to the contact of kind and joyful people, and have bright and uplifting conversations. When in doubt, notice how you feel after spending time with certain people. You will then know who to avoid.

Making gratitude a habit brings a lot of joy. If we look into our lives, it's certain we will find lots of things to be grateful for. With practice we can even be grateful for things we've been denied, and which would have been disastrous had they been given.

Feeling we have been helpful to someone also brings a lot of joy, whether it is an act as simple as giving directions to a stranger, or something more demanding in terms of time or energy. Helping others isn't always easy, especially when it involves family members or close friends, as we will see in the next point. That's why we should also consider the simplest acts of kindness and sympathy towards strangers.

We live in a culture where action is valued above all else. In Buddhism, however, the value of intention surpasses that of action. This may seem strange, but it makes sense. When we rejoice in acts of kindness and altruism, even if they are not our own, we feel great joy. Buddhist teachings even say that the power of rejoicing equals that of action itself.

I have often found that feeling we've done the right thing, when faced with a difficult choice, can bring great satisfaction. By doing the right thing I mean remaining faithful to ethical principles and values like the ones promoted by the Buddha.

Last but not least, joy can be found in the simple things in life, such as a nice walk in nature, a good meal, a smile from a stranger or watching puppies playing and letting their simple, innocent joy infect us.

As everything becomes easier with practice, even if joy is difficult at first, over time it will become part of our way of being and will arise spontaneously.

TSERING PALDRON

Helping others

Everyone knows the Chinese saying: "Give a man a fish and you feed him for a day. Teach him how to fish and you feed him for a lifetime". Our attitude of love and compassion for others should be guided by this maxim. We need to keep in mind that the purpose is to help them to help themselves and not keeping them dependent. This doesn't mean, of course, that we can't support them for a while, but this situation should be temporary. It is important that we help them achieve happiness and free themselves from suffering not just in the short term, but forever. In other words, show them the need to avoid the causes of suffering and cultivate the causes of happiness.

Helping others is a lot more delicate than it might seem at first glance, and it is not just about giving in to whims or spoiling the people around us. This kind of help might just be a way of avoiding conflict or getting into the good graces of others. In other words, for the helper to reap some personal benefit. We often hear people complain about ingratitude. Although ingratitude is quite common, sometimes we are the ones who exercise our help unwisely. The more discreet and empowering our help is the better. And ultimately, the fewer expectations we have, the more certain we can be of our genuine and selfless motives. It is, for example, much healthier and more dignified to offer someone a job than to simply give them money. People who win the lottery, for example, tend to want to help their relatives by sharing the money they've won with them. This is generous and commendable, but it usually works out very badly. Most of the time, the beneficiaries of their generosity may be happy and grateful at first, but they quickly become dissatisfied and ask for more. Studies show that people who suddenly come into a lot of money and act in this way end up becoming incompatible with their family and friends and are soon reduced to destitution.

Whether our help is material, emotional or in other ways, it must be subtle, disinterested and sufficiently discreet and skilful not to arouse other people's passions and destructive instincts. It isn't just to save ourselves disappointment and heartache; it's also to avoid giving them the opportunity to be ungrateful or mean.

If we don't have children or a family to look after, we may feel that our scope for kindness and compassion is limited and that we have few human contacts to help. However, there are countless ways to help others. If we have free time, we can look for volunteer work. This is a situation that favours selfless love, as it is aimed at people we don't feel attached to and from whom we receive nothing in return, other than gratitude.

Some hospitals accept volunteers to visit patients, keep them company, help them eat or read them a book. In paediatric hospitals, there is also a lot that can be done for children and their parents. Elderly people may need assistance with daily tasks and certainly need company. Prisoners, drug addicts, the homeless, abused children and women, people in need, abandoned animals: there's no shortage of things we can do. There are countless charitable organisations that need volunteers. All we have to do is look for the type of help we feel we can give.

If direct contact with people scares you, know that charities also need people for back-office work. Administrative tasks and organisation skills are essential and contribute directly to aid work.

TSERING PALDRON

Finding balance

Implementing what has been said so far may seem like a monumental task, but we don't need to do everything at once: consistency allows us to achieve amazing results, a little at a time. The training proposed by the Buddha is not a miraculous, instant salvation. It is a patient work of transformation, made up of small steps. No matter our starting point, whether we are terribly self-centred or even a criminal, as long as we are sincerely and genuinely motivated to transform ourselves, nothing can stop us from doing so.

Among Buddha's monks there were some with daunting pasts. Angulimala, for example, whose name means Necklace of Little Fingers, killed 999 people and cut off their little fingers to wear them on a necklace around his neck. He would be considered a serial killer in today's terms. However, after his encounter with the Buddha, he practised the Dharma with such energy and conviction that he eventually attained liberation.

Although not so radical, the story of Anathapindika is often told as an example of how it is always possible to transform ourselves. Anathapindika was an immensely wealthy merchant who was very stingy. One day he came to see the Buddha and told him. "I really appreciate your teachings, I find them very inspiring. However, I don't think they're for me." "Why is that?" asked the Buddha, "Because you speak so much about generosity and I can't imagine giving anything away."

"Do you think you could give a gift to yourself?" asked the Buddha. "I think so," he replied. The Buddha then suggested that every day he practise giving a gift, anything small, from one hand to another, saying *accept this* repeating the gesture as many times as possible. Anathapindika did so and, after a month, when it had become very easy and natural, he met the Buddha again, who gave him another exercise. This time he suggested he would set apart a small portion of the food he didn't like on his plate, to offer it later to a beggar or an animal. Little by little, he became more and more generous until he was nicknamed Anathapindika, which means *He who feeds the orphans and the poor*. His greatest fault became his greatest strength and it is said that he was the most generous of Buddha's disciples.

If both Angulimala and Anathapindika transformed themselves, so can we, as long as we are as sincere and determined as they were. Of course, change isn't easy and requires determination and effort. However, if we try too hard, we become irritable and intolerant of ourselves and others. It's essential to find the right balance. Too much effort never lasts long. Sometimes people get carried away and turn their lives upside down overnight, forcing themselves and others into acts and attitudes that aren't yet natural for them. But when the enthusiasm wears off, they abandon everything just as easily as they joined in. Other people never get started, pondering on a decision or an attitude to take. Avoiding doing too much or too little, the right attitude is one of persevering application, a constancy without tension, like that of a marathon runner.

What we need to do is start by clarifying what we want to achieve. If the Buddha's path makes sense to us and we are committed to the personal transformation necessary to follow it, then that becomes the main goal of our life to which we give our all. This doesn't mean that we should abandon our responsibilities and go live in a cave or a monastery, but rather consider our activities, experiences and attitudes as part of our training. It's not about fitting the spiritual path into our life, but about making our life a spiritual training.

Of course, there will always be ups and downs, moments of greater enthusiasm and others of some discouragement. It is important every day to redefine what we want to achieve, remind ourselves of our goals and rekindle our motivation. Traditionally, it's recommended that we renew our motivation once in the morning and once in the evening. In the morning, before we start the day, we remind ourselves of the purpose of transforming ourselves and consider all the day's activities as opportunities to implement new attitudes or correct old habits.

You can come up with a personal formula to express this, for example: "May I be able to create harmony today, harm no one and help in every way I can." You can also use more conventional formulas such as the stanza from the Buddhist Refuge or the Four Boundless Thoughts - you'll find them at the end of the book. But whatever the formula, the important thing is that we use it as if it were our own words, coming from the bottom of our heart.

In the evening, after a few moments of meditation, we can review our day, congratulate ourselves on what went well and acknowledge what didn't, without judgement or blame. We review the worst moments of our day and reflect on how we could have done better. Then reiterate our purpose for the next day and get ready for a restful night's sleep.

If we combine these two moments with a few moments of mindfulness during the day, we'll not only be able to stay motivated, but also sane in the midst of the endless tasks and demands that increasingly keep us under pressure.

An easy way to do this is simply to take a moment - whenever you remember - to take three conscious breaths. Wherever you are, whatever position you're in, while you're waiting for the light to turn green, the computer to start up, or any other situation, you can tune into a state of full awareness and hold it for three breaths. At the end of this book you'll find a more elaborate explanation of this instant meditation practice that doesn't interfere with anything and can change your life.

It's important to create a routine. Although the word has a negative connotation for many, of something mechanical or boring, there are also good routines. Making a habit of these pauses–the length of which depends on the time we have available–is a good example of a structure on which to base our practice and which will be a valuable help in maintaining continuity in times of discouragement.

Even if we manage to keep it up for a long time, sometimes we will feel an unwillingness to do anything. We then need to assess whether it's safe to take a break or whether it's still too risky. Taking a break can be invigorating and allow for a fresh start with renewed enthusiasm, at other times, it can be an open door to losing the benefits we've created at great cost over weeks and months. We must be able to judge for ourselves the best course of action. A few times a year it is good to refresh our motivation. Attending a retreat, going on a pilgrimage or simply taking a day or a few hours to relax, do some reading, go for a walk by the sea or in nature can be fundamental. Going for weekend retreats or seminars is a good way to renew our motivation. Hearing new perspectives, socialising with people who have similar goals, out of our usual context can allow us to regain strength and come back with redoubled enthusiasm.

Practical tips from chapter 3:

- Interdependence is structural, so that our happiness is inseparable from the happiness of others.
- The intelligent egoist is altruistic.
- Come out from behind your walls.
- All well-being depends on others.
- Be compassionate without fear.
- Rejoice in simple things.
- Wish well with no hope of return.
- Help others with wisdom.
- Your worst fault can become your best quality.
- Be persevering.
- Start each day with a positive intention and take stock at the end of the day.
- Take three conscious breaths every time you remember during the day

• CHAPTER 4 •

THE TRUTH OF SUFFERING

We live in a society where the realities of life are systematically swept under the carpet. The dead are made up for funerals; the effects of age are disguised with Botox; unhappiness is masked with antidepressants; the disabled are hidden away in institutions; odours are lessened with air fresheners. Anything that doesn't convey the idea that life is full of bright promises, that we will always be fit, young and healthy is methodically removed from our eyes so that we can continue our rosy nightmare.

We think it's easier to pretend that everything is fine rather than deal with reality and we do our best to keep busy and avoid confrontation. And everything is so well organised that we always have something to distract ourselves with if something painful happens. For the rest, we escape the banality of our own lives by living by proxy through reality shows and soap operas, vibrating with fictional emotions experienced fictionally by fictional characters and thus keeping the inescapable truths of our human condition out of our field of vision. Perhaps in hope that not seeing them or thinking about them will make them disappear.

The problem is that this doesn't happen and, when we least expect it, life confronts us with hardships. Then, because we're totally unprepared and our usual distraction strategies no longer work, we are lost and desperate, not knowing where to turn or what to do. Whether we like it or not, suffering is inherent in the way we experience the world. Distracting ourselves from this reality doesn't make it go away, so the best thing we can do is face it. That's what Buddha did 2,500 years ago.

The truth of suffering

Buddha was a human being like us. Although he lived in a very different time, his aspiration for well-being and his fear of suffering were the same. But, unlike most of us, instead of trying to distract himself from thinking about these things, Buddha looked into the anxieties and fears of humanity and asked himself some fundamental questions.

This essential issue was the theme for his first teaching. This teaching, which became known as *The Four Noble Truths* and is the foundation of all Buddhist teachings, is the answer to four essential questions: What is suffering? What causes it? Is it possible to eradicate it and, if so, how?

The word used by the Buddha in his presentation was *dukkha*, which has been translated as suffering but doesn't mean exactly that. *Dukkha* means frustration or dissatisfaction rather than suffering. This distinction is important because when the Buddha says that everything is *dukkha*, the translation everything is suffering conveys a dark and pessimistic approach that doesn't correspond to the original meaning. Even if we recognise that life isn't always easy, to say that everything in life is suffering seems an overstatement. In fact, what we call suffering is the visible aspect of *dukkha*, the physical or mental pain of being confronted with something we don't want or losing something we value. And, fortunately, it's not constant.

However, if we go back to the original meaning, saying that everything is unsatisfactory seems to make a lot more sense. We all have felt dissatisfaction. Of course, when something doesn't satisfy us, we think it's because it's not perfect for us and there is something else that will fulfil us. That's why we jump from relationship to relationship, job to job, house to house. An irrational and often unconscious hope guides our choices, making us believe, even after five divorces, that the *right* person is still out there.

When Buddha shared his conclusions, he began by stating what he called the truth of suffering. And what is this truth? The dissatisfaction we feel is not the result of any imperfection in external objects, it is a deep-seated feeling and, therefore, no external object can eliminate it. Of course, there are emotional or material factors that contribute to our well-being, but external factors are too unstable for us to rely on them exclusively. For a period, we can enjoy a satisfying love relationship, a successful professional career and an enviable social status. But we don't know for how long. Not only can these conditions suddenly change, but we ourselves may find that they no longer fulfil us.

If we depend entirely on these factors, we live in terror that they will deteriorate, and we try to control people and situations so that they never fail us. This puts us in a state of great vulnerability and automatically generates fear, desire and aversion, as well as all the negative emotions that further erode and destroy our well-being.

What Buddha wanted to point out was that not only can we not obtain lasting happiness and well-being by relying on external conditions, but the fact that we exclusively depend on them feeds fears and desires that disturb our peace of mind. Convinced that happiness depends on an object or a person, what drastic measures will we go to in order to secure them? What situations will we put ourselves in? And conversely, if we believe that an object or person is the cause of our suffering, how far will we go to remove them from our life?

So, it's important to realise that Buddha doesn't mean to deny the value or influence that external conditions have on our well-being. What he means is that, since dissatisfaction is internal and, in a way, inherent to our state of mind, external objects cannot remedy it. Furthermore, because of the instability of the world, when we rely solely on external conditions to achieve happiness, it is impossible to achieve lasting peace.

Therefore, if we want to enjoy well-being and harmony, we must cultivate them within ourselves and not depend exclusively on events or situations. The conditions we talked about in previous chapters—a healthy and balanced lifestyle, ethics and positive emotions—help us to create a balanced and stable inner structure and to depend less on situations.

The causes of suffering

Thus, according to Buddha, dissatisfaction and suffering are caused by the limitations of our own mind. We don't understand the reality of life, being constantly confused about the nature of the world and of ourselves. This confusion in which we are immersed generates a lot of insecurity and is the ideal breeding ground for the destructive feelings that agitate and confuse us even more. Buddha's enquiry into the nature of his own mind led him to draw enlightening conclusions about the origin of the insecurity we all feel.

It all begins with the way we identify with the thoughts and emotions that stir within us. Since our attention is totally absorbed by them, and they are deeply volatile, never remaining for more than a few fleeting moments, the result is an inner turmoil similar to the waves on the surface of the ocean that never stop moving. In this state, we are inattentive and disconnected from the deeper, more stable stream of consciousness, which we access relatively easily as soon as we learn to rest our minds in the present moment. Experiencing this stream, even briefly, is felt as a deep underlying stillness, silent and serene.

Since we're not used to connecting with it, we turn to the outside world in search of stability, and the more so since objects seem solid and trustworthy to us... We couldn't be more wrong! The solidity we see is just an illusion, a projection that we superimpose on reality, in the desperate search for the certainty and stability that we can't find within ourselves. Perhaps this explains why, in both the infinitely large and the infinitely small, everything is practically empty and only in our dimension does it solidify. Whatever the case, we fervently want the material world to be solid, stable and reliable so that we can hold on to it during inner storms. Unfortunately, that doesn't work.

The classic Buddhist texts, written centuries ago, teach us that the material world is unreliable. With only the microscope of their mind, Buddhist meditators didn't need modern equipment to realise that the material world, being made up of almost non-existent particles (or waves) and always in motion, couldn't offer the stability and permanence we seek. An important part of our suffering comes precisely from seeing our expectations of security dashed. We project a world in which we expect everything be coherent, stable, permanent, independent and solid, but we find the opposite: phenomena are unstable, impermanent, fluctuating and totally interdependent. That's why, when we lose something, when a situation changes, or when, in one way or another, we are confronted with the impermanence of phenomena, we feel it as a threat to our stability. The phenomena are just expressing their nature–it's us who panic because we don't want them to be like that.

The three types of dukkha

Traditionally, Buddhism recognises three types of *dukkha*. The first–as we've already seen–is the obvious suffering of, for example, falling ill, growing old or losing a loved one. This type of *dukkha* happens whenever we are confronted with something we don't want and produces physical or emotional pain that needs no explanation because it is too obvious. This type of suffering is easily recognised by everyone.

The second is the *dukkha* of impermanence, the anxiety or stress that results from things always changing. This level of *dukkha*, which is more subtle, only becomes apparent when we look into it. At first glance, certain objects seem desirable as sources of well-being. Indeed, when we obtain them, they undoubtedly produce some short-term pleasure. However, over time, everything that gives us pleasure can bring us pain, when it changes, when it ceases, when we lose interest or simply fear that it will change or disappear. This type of *dukkha* includes the desire to obtain certain things, the frustration of not being able to get them and, when we do, the stress of keeping them and the fear of losing them.

The third type is omnipresent *dukkha*, the feeling of dissatisfaction resulting from things never living up to our expectations: they don't last, they're not stable, and they're not solid or reliable. When we are more inexperienced, we tend to rely completely on external objects and situations. That's why a teenager's first heartbreak is so devastating: it's possibly the first time that the nature of internal and external phenomena lets us down. After a few painful experiences, we become clearer about what the world can offer and perhaps begin to feel existential angst. What's the point of all this, anyway, if you can't trust anything?

In societies where basic needs are not met, the first two levels of *dukkha* produce the most suffering. Today in our society, existential anguish, stress, fear and the lack of meaning in life are just as devastating, if not more so. On the one hand, this is an interesting situation in that it predisposes us towards generating interest in these teachings and understanding them better. For us, learning to deal with suffering not only consists of dealing with the first two levels of *dukkha*, suffering and impermanence, but also with constant unease, frustration, and meaninglessness.

Conflicting emotions

Our dependence on external phenomena as a source of stability and security puts us in a very difficult situation. Nothing we experience is left as it is. As we are always in an acute state of self-preservation, constantly seeking to solidify and strengthen our sense of self, anything that seems to strengthen it is seen as desirable and anything that appears to weaken it is seen as dangerous. What's more, in this state of emergency, it's difficult to see things clearly and so the way we assess phenomena is often hasty and arbitrary, based on habit, on what we have learnt from our parents, or from the people around us.

When something is judged to be desirable, we feel an urgent need to make it our own, to incorporate it into our sense of self. Whether it's a person or an object, a quality, a status, a privilege of any kind: it becomes urgent to obtain it. This is how something that was totally indifferent to us in one moment becomes indispensable to our survival an instant later. This grasping impulse, often referred to as *desire* or *attachment* in the Buddhist context, is one of the basic conflicting emotions, or *kleshas*, and one of the most fundamental causes of suffering. Under its influence, the object of our desire is seen as endowed with all the qualities and requirements to enhance the feeling of *I*, and we don't hesitate to resort to any method to obtain it—often negative actions of which we will have to bear the consequences.

Conversely, when something is judged to be undesirable or threatening, we want to get rid of it, destroy it if possible. We feel a deep aversion and see only flaws and imperfections in that object. As with attachment, aversion also blinds us to reality and triggers powerful emotions that often translate into disastrous actions.

The greater the feelings of insecurity and instability, the greater the blindness and the more intense the emotions, the greater will be the turmoil of our mind. It's a vicious circle. Thus, unawareness of the deepest and most stable levels of consciousness is what puts us in a state of chronic alienation and imbalance from which everything else comes forth. Buddha called it *avidhya* (*marigpa*, in Tibetan) or unconsciousness and pointed to it as the origin of all suffering, from the most subtle levels of *dukkha* to the visible suffering that we all know and fear.

But if suffering is inherent in this way of functioning, is it possible to free ourselves from it? The Buddha's answer is yes. *Avidhya* is not an inevitable condition, but merely an accidental state of unawareness. The vicious cycle that sets in, however, makes it difficult to recognise the deeper, more subtle levels of the mind because our attention is always drawn to the surface, where thoughts and emotions churn.

We have to appease our mind thanks to an ethical and healthy lifestyle and, at the same time, learn to divert our attention away from thoughts and emotions and let it return to the inner natural stillness. This is precisely the aim of the training that Buddha outlined.

This honest approach of suffering might be seen by some as a bit gloomy. Of course, it contradicts the rosy view that everything always ends well and conveys a somehow different reality: as long as we haven't dispelled the misunderstanding about who we are and what the world is, we are prone to suffer.

The reality of life

Our society's rejection of suffering has almost turned it into a taboo. Expectations of success, well-being and pleasure are such that when we can't fulfil them, we think something is wrong with us. When we look around us, we might believe that we are surrounded by happy and successful people. But the reality is that many of them hide their suffering under layers of anxiety meds and antidepressants. Paradoxically, when we realise the reality of suffering, we feel great relief. It's normal to feel *dukkha*, in all its forms, and we don't have to feel bad about suffering.

One of the things that shocks us most about countries like India is that there, unlike in most of Europe, suffering is there for all to see. The lepers, the homeless, the blind, the beggars and the disabled are not hidden away in specialised institutions: they are there for all to see, constantly reminding us that pain, suffering, illness and death are inevitable. All these things are experienced as realities and not as plagues or anomalies. They are neither hidden nor dramatised. They are simply real.

GROW YOUR OWN HAPPINESS

I remember my first trip to Nepal in 1989. When the aeroplane doors opened with the first breath of air, a mixture of very real and contradictory smells reached my nostrils: spices, damp earth, flowers and sewage. It was a whole olfactory image of what awaited me. In general, we Westerners don't know how to react to such realism. I have friends who couldn't get out of the airport and stayed in India just long enough to catch a flight home. Seeing the misery, disease and lack of conditions is uncomfortable, of course. Only a heart of stone isn't shaken by the hungry stares with which the beggars attentively follow our every bite. But I suspect that it's not just our compassion that is put to the test. The suffering of others bothers us—it's natural and healthy for it to do so, it's a sign that we're not totally shielded. But what also bothers us is that we have before our eyes the painful realities that are usually hidden and that we prefer to ignore. We are more concerned with pleasure and well-being and don't want anything to spoil that. When confronted with the suffering of others, most of us close ourselves off and reject it so that our own well-being isn't jeopardised. On the other hand, we are so unfamiliar with it that we are uncomfortable and don't know how to react.

In India, however, we are thrown to the lions. There, the realities of life are not just in plain sight: they are exposed and exploited for begging so that there is no escaping them. Wherever we go, we are pursued by them and constantly confronted with our inability to respond adequately.

Ringu Tulku often recounts that when he started visiting the West, he was perplexed by the problems he was confronted with by the people who asked to speak to him. Like many Tibetans of his generation, Ringu Tulku travelled for months to escape persecution by the Chinese army. Many of his group didn't survive and only a small number made it to India. On arrival, the brutal difference in temperature and climate exposed them to unknown diseases which, combined with the extremely precarious conditions of survival and hygiene, decimated many of the survivors.

On one of his first visits to the West, someone asked to see him. He sat down looking very unhappy and said he'd come to say goodbye. "Are you going away?" asked Rinpoche. "No, I'm going to commit suicide; my life has ceased to make sense since my wife left me." This answer left Ringu Tulku perplexed. But instead of trying to dissuade him, he told him. "There are many women in the world, but I understand. However, I'd like to suggest that before you kill yourself you take a two-month trip to India."

It was the other man's turn to be mystified: "Two months? I can't afford that!" Rinpoche smiled, with his characteristic mischievous air, and replied: "That's no argument. If you're going to kill yourself anyway, what do you need your savings for?"

A few months later, the man returned. He was totally transformed, smiling and his face lit up. "I took your advice," he said as soon as he sat down. Rinpoche smiled. "And the journey went well?" "Beautifully! Well, I was ill for a week, with intestinal fever. It was a nightmare, I had to go to hospital and I lost twenty pounds. But I'm very happy!" "Is that so? And why is that?" asked Rinpoche. "Because I realised how lucky I am! When I saw how those people live, I realised I have all the conditions to be happy!" A trip to India can be such a therapy for Westerners who, like us, have lost sight of the harsh realities of life!

Of course, suffering and happiness are always comparative evaluations. When we compare ourselves with the bigger picture around us, we can consider ourselves fortunate or unfortunate and feel unhappier than necessary or, on the contrary, minimise our complaints. It all depends on our point of comparison. There are always those around us who are better off and those who are worse off. And even if the levels of well-being, essentially material, in the Western world are much higher than in poor countries, the truth is that we can't be fooled by appearances. Our hospitals are cleaner, but that doesn't mean that the patients who are hospitalised there aren't suffering.

I don't think we should avoid confronting the reality of life. I hear people say that they haven't been to visit a friend or family member who is ill because they can't bear to see their state of degradation and want to remember them as they used to be. It's understandable, but I suspect the truth is different and perhaps not so pretty. Because the suffering of others bothers us, it's not easy to get close to those who are in pain. We feel it as a potential threat—it could be happening to us! This reminder of reality makes us very uncomfortable. We are unaccustomed to living with suffering and we feel such rejection that we react as if we saw a scorpion crawling up our leg.

This lack of coexistence and openness towards the things that are an integral part of our condition ends up making us inhuman and means that we don't know what to do or say in the face of suffering and pain. This creates a heavy and uncomfortable atmosphere in which we avoid talking about what's really important and opt for trivial matters. And, in the end, the worst thing of all is that this hypocrisy leads to increasing alienation and frightening desensitisation. We think we can protect ourselves from suffering by ignoring it, but in fact we condemn ourselves to walking through life like robots and soothing the underlying anguish with medication, excluding any chance of true happiness. Because by not wanting to feel suffering we can no longer feel anything else.

It's no coincidence that anyone who travels to poorer countries notices how, paradoxically, the most disadvantaged people there don't look unhappy. Dominique Lapierre, a French writer and reporter for Paris-Match magazine, spent some time living in the slums of Calcutta. It was this experience that inspired his novel *La cité de la joie (The City of Joy)*, from which a film was made (*The City of Joy* by Ronald Joffé with Patrick Swayze). In the introduction, he writes: "In the heart of this hell I find more heroism, more love, more sharing and, finally, more joy than in many cities of our opulent West. I meet people who have nothing and who in the end have everything. In the midst of so much ugliness, so much sadness, so much mud and so much rubbish, I discover more beauty and more hope than in many paradises here. And above all, I discover that this inhuman city has the magical power to create saints."

Of course, this is not to suggest that poverty is healthy or desirable. It would be great if humanity stood up to put an end to injustice, discrimination and social inequalities, if the richest countries applied the material means at their disposal to eliminating misery where it exists. My point is that the more aware we are of the realities of life, the more prepared we will be to face them and the less we will react like spoilt kids in difficult times.

Acceptance, the non-violent approach

One of the great problems when facing suffering is our violent rejection of it. It's not just that we don't want to suffer; we have a real phobia, an uncontrollable aversion to suffering. So, when something unpleasant happens, there is the primary, direct suffering caused by the fact itself, the secondary, indirect suffering that comes from speculation, fear and anguish, and underlying these two is the violent rejection of any kind of suffering. This aversion is a major source of aggravation.

The longer we remain stuck in rejection, the longer we put off relieving suffering. The intense aversion we feel takes up all the space and prevents us from finding solutions and implementing improvements. Hatred blinds us and we don't realise that by giving in to it, we are making our situation substantially worse. That's why the first step towards lessening our suffering is acceptance. It may seem paradoxical because, intuitively, we have the feeling that rejection protects us from the undesirable and therefore fear that acceptance will make us more vulnerable. But this isn't true. Does resisting something that has happened ever stop it from happening or move it out of our way?

Acceptance begins as a mere acknowledgement of the situation, viewing it objectively, getting to know it better, exploring it in all its contrasting aspects and looking at it from different angles. It is important to realise that acceptance doesn't mean that we agree, acquiesce or collaborate with what has happened. Nor does it mean that we give up doing anything, but rather that we are finally ready to work with what happened.

Conversely, denial means we want to maintain the illusion that everything is fine, that if we close our eyes everything will be as it was before, that we can still wake up and discover that it was all just a bad dream. Most of us probably go through this phase when faced with a difficult situation. In a healthy process, sooner or later we surrender to the evidence: what happened has happened and there's no going back. And we can finally deal with the situation.

However, if we persist in non-acceptance, we close ourselves off and become blocked, which generates terrible tension. This tension, which we mistakenly think is generated by the situation, is actually created by rejection and only makes everything worse without bringing any solution. Over time, rejection can lead to bitterness and anger. We feel separated from others more than ever and we spy on them out of the corner of our eye, railing against their indifference: "How can you smile and feel happy? Can't you see how much I'm suffering?" We feel forsaken, discriminated against and can enter a state of paranoia and obsession where there is no room for anything else.

If we are aware of the inevitable nature of suffering, acceptance might be easier. It's not as if all around us is joy and well-being and we are the only ones suffering. Of course, as we've already seen, we live in a society that rejects and hides suffering and therefore, if we don't look more closely, it might seem that everyone is happy and content. But deep down we all know that's not true.

Acceptance can therefore arise when we distance ourselves from our problems enough to be able to look around us. Then we inevitably realise that, in one way or another, everyone suffers, that suffering is part of life. And so, instead of getting angry, thinking that what happens to us is unfair, we humbly and openly recognise that if it has happened to so many other people, why shouldn't it happen to us?

Acceptance is achieved in stages and is an ongoing process. The more painful the situation we're facing, the more we'll have to go backwards and forwards. There may be a real war raging inside us, during which we will win some battles and lose others. But the important thing is to progressively accept the different aspects of our situation, saving what can be saved, resolving and improving what we have left and learning to accept what cannot be changed.

Nothing happens by chance

Few of us are able to accept suffering and open up to it immediately. Unless we are very well trained, acceptance is a process that takes time. Some people feel that trying to understand the situation they are in and making sense of it can help them to accept it better. It is true that, sometimes, understanding paves the way for acceptance. Thus, it can be useful to investigate what caused this painful event. Not in the sense of assigning blame, but in order to place it in a wider context and dispel the tension created by thinking that everything revolves around us.

Since the way phenomena exist is through interdependence, whatever the situation, it didn't come out of nowhere. We weren't targeted or randomly chosen to face this suffering; it's neither the result of chance nor a whim of providence. If we reflect on the links of causality and interdependence implicit in any situation, we immediately have a much broader vision. It's easy to realise that there are always many other people involved, many choices for which we are responsible, and that it would have only taken one different circumstance for the outcome to have been different.

If we want to analyse what led to a road accident, for example, we'll see that there are a large number of causes. Driver A left home late and in a hurry, angry at having had an argument with his wife. He was driving fast, distracted, thinking about the argument he'd just had and annoyed at being late for a professional meeting. Driver B was driving at his usual time, on an everyday route, but he had forgotten his sunglasses and was facing the sun. When he realised there was a pothole in the road, he tried to avoid it, but his car spun out of control and hit the other car. If we go deeper, we'll discover other causes, for example, the reason for driver A's marital difficulties, the reason why driver B forgot his glasses, driver A's choleric temperament, driver B's carelessness, etc. If we analyse carefully, we will find in this event the outcome of causal processes that began weeks or months before.

Little by little, the image of the event grows, set in a much wider context: the hole in the road should have been repaired by now, but due to the negligence of the relevant service, it hadn't been repaired. The causes of this negligence, in turn, lead to problems of hierarchy and relationships between service personnel, issues of bureaucracy and corruption in the town hall. The mayor, the minister, the government, the election campaign and its priorities may all be involved. Broadening our vision, we get a picture on a local, national or global scale and see that this accident didn't come out of nowhere but was the culmination of a set of dynamic processes involving many people and extending over time.

Sometimes, intuitively, people express this by saying that "nothing happens by chance". But it's important to realise that this doesn't mean what happened was predestined, programmed to happen as an independent event.

Nothing happens by chance because everything is the result, the culmination, of various intricate causal processes and is therefore neither random nor programmed: it happens due to the coming together of causes and circumstances. For instance, if we want to make a hard-boiled egg, we need an egg, a pan, water and a source of heat, and we need those things to remain present for around 10 minutes. If anything is missing, or if we can't get them to stay for that long we cannot achieve the intended result. But then, on the other hand, if all the necessary things are gathered and remain present for the necessary length of time, there is no way the egg will not be hard-boiled.

This simple example has numerous implications and understanding it can make all the difference in enabling us to break down - and finally accept–a difficult situation that has arisen. Firstly, it may be useful to explain what is meant by causes and circumstances. Causes are the substantial causes, the element or factor that provides the substance for the result. In our example, the substantial cause is the egg. Circumstances are the circumstantial causes that allow the transformation process to take place: the water, the heat source, the pan, the time during which the egg is subjected to that temperature, etc.

When we say that nothing happens by chance, we are realising that all the necessary causes and circumstances had to come together for that result to occur. On the other hand, when we say that it was meant to happen, we are somehow realising that, given those conditions, it was impossible for the outcome to be any different. It isn't always obvious that we have a clear understanding of this. Most of the time we feel, intuitively and in a somewhat confused way, that there is a logic behind life's events, that they are not merely random.

Another issue that often plagues us is the feeling that a certain event is unfair. Not necessarily that it's unfair in itself, but that it's unfair that it should happen to us. "Why me? Why me?" These is the question we ask ourselves. According to the Buddhist perspective, nothing that happens is fair or unfair, it just happens through the combination of different causes. This part is relatively easy to understand and even accept. But why does it happen to us? This is where things get tricky.

Karma, the causality of actions

Causality, as the mechanical law that makes the world work, is relatively easy to observe around us. Of course, when we start looking into these issues, we quickly realise that causal processes are extremely complex. Even something as simple as boiling an egg involves such a large number of causes that we could almost say they relate to everything. This is what the Buddha meant by interdependence being the way things exist.

But these causal processes don't just concern the material world. Our inner world and our experiences also exist in interdependence with countless factors. In Buddhism we call *karma* the specific aspect of the law of causality that establishes a relationship between actions and beings' experiences of happiness and suffering.

The word *karma* means action, indicating that it is our physical, verbal and mental actions that condition our experience of the world. What this means is that the positive or negative nature of everything we do, say or think influences the positive or negative nature of our experiences. In a way, the world that each of us experiences is a projection of our own, which is why we can share the same space with someone and experience it completely differently. Everything that happens to us is our own experience and therefore happens *within us*. Often, when we think something is unfair, it's because we don't think we did anything to *deserve* a certain outcome. Firstly, whatever happens isn't a retribution but a consequence and secondly, we are rarely aware of the impact of what we do.

We often think we've never hurt anyone. It is true that very few people deliberately intend to harm others. In most cases we think we are only preserving our interests—even when we hurt others—and consider it to be perfectly legitimate. Driven by self-centredness and with only our own well-being in mind, we act out of hatred, attachment and other destructive emotions, harming or hurting others. But, because we are blinded by those strong emotions, we are generally unable to recognise our mistakes and always tend to think that it is someone else's fault. When we understand the law of karma, we at least realise that, even if we don't see how, we can be sure that everything that happens in our life has something to do with us, which isn't the same as saying that it's our fault. This distinction is fundamental because it's not a question of fault, be it ours or others.

When we feel attacked and react angrily, we think we're just defending ourselves. If we act on that anger and punch someone, for example, we will have to face the consequences. Even if it's easy enough to understand, we often refuse to take responsibility for our actions and feel they are unfair because we were provoked in the first place. It's important to note that it's not the fact that we defend ourselves that is a problem, but the fact that we feel anger. If we are attacked, it is natural and appropriate to defend ourselves. If we don't do it in anger, we might act in a way that, for example, only neutralises our attacker, but if we do it in anger, we tend to overreact. It's the difference between responding and reacting.

The primary factor in karma is the intention or emotion that moves us. Actions, whether physical or verbal, act as aggravating circumstances. The place, the moment, the person who is at the receiving end of our action, our relationship with that person, the circumstances, the intensity of the emotion etc. are all variables that determine different degrees of karmic impact.

All these karmas act like potential vulnerabilities. What do I mean by vulnerability? Think about how the immune system works. Germs, bacteria and viruses are around us at all times but a good immune system will shield us from them very effectively. If something in our body comes out of balance it may create vulnerability in the immune system that will allow a virus to penetrate. In a similar way, a pure ethical conduct shields us from most of the harm that surrounds us, but negative actions create vulnerabilities that allow in the negative results that align with them.

In a prison in the United States, an experiment was carried out in which prisoners serving sentences for theft and robbery were shown a short film showing people walking down the street, and asked to identify the victims they would choose for a robbery. The results were surprising: almost all the prisoners chose the same victims. Thinking it might have something to do with that population or that region of the country they decided to extend the experiment and conducted it in other prisons in other cities. The results were identical. Although the prisoners couldn't say precisely what made them choose those people over others, there seemed to be unanimity in recognising certain signs that would make them easier prey.

In the same way, it's as if we unconsciously always carry the sum of all our vulnerabilities, potentially exposing ourselves to them. However, they remain latent and only manifest when all the necessary circumstances come together. In the example above, the people identified carried some kind of vulnerability, but that doesn't mean that they were robbed. The necessary circumstances need to come together and, until they do, this won't happen. However, like in the example of the hard-boiled egg, the moment all the causes and circumstances gather there is no way the result will not manifest, even if it is many lifetimes later.

Understanding responsibility

I have a friend who makes a habit of paying all his bills on the last day. He's not a dishonest person and always pays what he owes, but usually only on the last day of the term. But once it cost him. My friend had a bill of 1,500 Euros to pay to the tax office and, as usual, he put it off until the last day. And that day, when he sat down to make the transfer, he realised that his wife's credit card payment had fallen through and the account didn't have enough funds. The banks had already closed, all internet transfers took a day or two, so there was nothing he could do. He resigned himself to the idea that he could still pay within a week with a ten per cent fine. And he let the week pass.

On the last day of the deadline, he sat down again to make the transfer. But this time the bank's website was down. And once again he couldn't pay. As he had a lawyer friend, he asked him to take care of the matter. More deadlines and more obstacles and the matter dragged on. As bad luck would have it, the friend, who had an important case in hand, missed another deadline, got the wrong document and the bill finally came: €5,000 to pay.

My friend was furious. He blamed his wife for spending without counting, the bank for having a disgraceful website and, ultimately, his lawyer friend for being incompetent. He got angry with everyone and, of course, had to pay more than 3 times the initial sum. It was easy to put the blame on the friend who had, in fact, been careless. The bank's website wasn't perfect and maybe the wife was a spendthrift, but he wouldn't have been forced to pay €5,000 if he had abandoned his habit of always paying on the last day!

Sometimes, when this kind of thing happens, we fixate on others' mistakes and make them responsible for our setbacks. But we forget to recognise that we were the ones who put ourselves in a vulnerable situation in the first place.

I always recall an interview with a Zen master that I read in a French magazine. The journalist asked him: "You Zen people have a reputation for being very calm and impassive, but are you always like that? How would you react, for example, if you were stuck in traffic on Place de l'Étoile at 2pm and had to catch a plane at Charles de Gaulle at 2.30pm?" The Zen master smiled and replied: "My dear friend, if I had to catch a plane at Charles de Gaulle at 2.30 pm, I would never be stuck in traffic on Place de l'Étoile at 2.00 pm!"

Like my friend, we often miss the opportunity to learn great lessons. Even when we suffer for other people's mistakes, there's always something that puts us at their mercy. That's why ethics is so important. It's not just a question of acting according to a set of moral principles; it is above all a question of acting fairly and appropriately, responding rather than reacting, which also safeguards and protects us from other people's mistakes. However, as I've already mentioned, it's very possible that the way in which a certain event in our lives is linked to our responsibility is not very clear. This may be due, on the one hand, to the fact that we are quite unconscious of our behaviour and, on the other, to the fact that certain karmas were created at a time we no longer remember.

From the Buddhist point of view, consciousness is an uninterrupted flow that can stream through successive lives and, therefore, it is possible that certain events that seem to have no relation to our present existence are the consequences of actions carried out in other lives. Of course, this concept is completely foreign to our culture and therefore perhaps it doesn't make any sense to you. I have seen how the idea of successive lives, or rebirths, makes sense to some people and is violently rejected by others. I don't think it's appropriate, since that's not the subject, to deal with this issue here. I only mention it because there may be hidden factors that make it difficult to understand the causes of any given situation. Ultimately, although understanding can be liberating, it is not vital for acceptance.

Because of our cultural heritage, we may continue to think of suffering as punishment. Often, even after some understanding of the law of karma, we can't get rid of the idea that there is a hidden intention in the way the consequences of our actions manifest. Such an intention, of course, presupposes a judgemental power or providence, which distributes punishments and rewards based on a moral assessment of our actions. For Buddhism, there is no such thing as providence, just as there is no retributive intention in the way the law of karma works. It's just the mechanics of phenomena. However, the truth is that because suffering is the natural consequence of the karma we have created, if we had the ability to recognise it, our life would be one of constant learning.

In fact, if the causal process reached its ultimate consequences in a short time, we would probably all have abandoned negative actions. When we put our hand in the fire, we get burned. The causal link is easily recognised, and it only takes getting burned once to learn. If we put our hand in the fire and only got burnt after a year, it would be difficult to discern exactly what caused the burn and it would take several painful experiences before we learnt our lesson. It's the same with negative actions: when the result is swift, we see the connection, when it appears after many years, it's almost impossible to establish the cause.

As much as it pains us to admit it, suffering is a reminder of what is truly important in life. In difficult times, the order of priorities changes to something much closer to reality. Suddenly, peace of mind, health and affection become much more important than new shoes, a weekend away or a beach holiday. In normal times we don't always value the essential things and we get angry if something incidental doesn't go as we expect, but when we are suffering we immediately realise what's most important. That's why people who are going through difficult situations often value things that they hadn't noticed before. It's normal for them to reorganise their priorities and live much more in the present, without too many projects or expectations, much more attentive to the small joys and pleasures that usually pass them by.

Paradoxically, by rejecting the reality of suffering, we condemn ourselves to a superficial life and avoid any deeper feelings. Happiness is reduced to the satisfaction of short-term desires and life quickly loses its meaning. This explains why, in a society as affluent as ours, there is so much hidden unhappiness.

Practical tips from chapter 4:

- Suffering is part of life and inherent in our way of experiencing the world.
- Hiding and rejecting suffering only creates more anguish.
- Nothing happens by chance, all is the result of causes and conditions
- Karma is the aspect of causality applied to the results of our actions.
- Understand your responsibility even when others make mistakes.

• CHAPTER 5 •

BUILDING RESILIENCE

If we live according to what has been said in the previous chapters, we'll deal with everyday situations with more ease and our attitude will be calmer. We will have better relationships, far fewer conflicts, and our mind will be at peace. Even though with training we can maintain a positive attitude in increasingly challenging situations, there will be times when we face adverse circumstances, financial difficulties or illnesses. However, it is possible to face them without burdening ourselves with the unnecessary suffering caused by our reaction. We're usually unaware of the difference between the facts and our evaluation and reaction to them. For us, it's all about the situation and we can't see how we make ourselves suffer in a totally unnecessary way.

Naturally, some people are more prone to cogitation than others. Faced with the same kind of adverse circumstances, there are those who face them calmly and those who become so anxious that their appetite, sleep and health suffer. But regardless of our natural tendency, we can learn to manage the mental suffering caused by unnecessary speculation.

Quite often the suffering caused by the situation itself is much less than that generated by speculation or anticipation. Others can hurt us, physically or verbally, for a while and to a certain extent, but there is no limit to the torment our mind inflicts on us. The bully goes home at the end of the day and forgets we exist. But our uncontrolled mind keeps his bullying with us whilst we eat, sleep, spend the weekend or go on holiday. We try to avoid our enemies, keep them under control or subdue them, but we forget that our own mind can be the most ruthless of all. The good news is that it doesn't have to be this way.

Accept the setback

Sometimes the possibility that something won't go according to our wishes is enough to make us angry, anxious and restless. It can give us a sleepless night, mentally weaving a dreadful scenario. But we can train to react differently by accepting small setbacks. When something doesn't go as we expected, before we lose patience or panic, we should stop and consider whether what is happening is worrying or simply different from what we anticipated. We often react because something goes against our expectations and not because it's actually a problem.

Very often, we get stuck by thinking something is wrong and shouldn't happen; that the people involved are acting badly, unethically or disrespectfully. We get so stuck in this opinion that we fail to try to solve the situation and prolong the suffering unnecessarily.

A few years ago, I had neighbours who threw parties every weekend until the early hours of the morning: they had friends over, played cards and blasted loud music. My bedroom was right below their living room, so it was impossible to sleep. After a few tormented weekends, I realised that what was stopping me from sleeping wasn't so much the decibels as my thoughts of indignation. There was more shouting inside me than music upstairs: "How is it possible to have so little respect for others? Do they think they're alone in the world?" Weekends became a nightmare, but not only then. I found myself dreading on Monday the noise they were going to make on Friday. At that point I realised that I was letting the situation take over my life and that urgent action had to be taken.

This realisation is difficult but essential. Otherwise, any situation can become a nightmare, eventually leading to violence, depression or paranoia. We must be able to deal with the situation, leaving aside our reaction to it. I'd already asked them to turn down the volume, I'd already called the police. What else could I do to stop the noise? Nothing. I wondered then if there was anything I could do to minimise the inconvenience and several options came to mind: moving into a different bedroom, sleeping on the sofa in the living room at weekends or putting in earplugs. In the end, I opted for the third option and was finally able to rest.

Sometimes we get so trapped in righteousness that we fail to find a practical solution and unnecessarily prolong the suffering. All along I was thinking "I'm not sleeping on the couch because of these jerks!", "I'm not putting in earplugs, *they* have to shut up!" or other similar things, I was putting off easy and simple solutions that didn't require their goodwill.

Once I managed to minimise the noise, it was easier to calm the indignation. Obviously, the situation wasn't ideal; obviously they had no respect for others; obviously it would be normal they stopped making noise by 12am. But there was nothing more I could do, and I had to find a way to make my life easier.

We must realise that no matter how right we are, things are just what they are and there is no guarantee that they will be fair, predictable or controllable. We should try to accept the situation as it is, openly and calmly, and adjust to reality as quickly as possible, instead of creating additional stress. After all, irritation and impatience won't solve anything; they just make the situation worse. The smart thing to do is to relax and focus our energy on solving it rather than complicating it unnecessarily.

Once we manage to deal with life's normal setbacks, we begin to be able to deal with more delicate situations without adding unnecessary problems. When we look closely, many of the dramas we experience daily are nothing more than minor setbacks that we let escalate to dramatic proportions. We also must understand that accepting situations doesn't mean agreeing with them, but just recognising that they are what they are. Of course, this doesn't stop us from trying to solve the external situation insofar as there is a solution. If there isn't then we all we can do is to adapt, minimise the damage and not block ourselves with the fact that we are right. Situations don't need our permission to happen, the world doesn't exist according to what we think is fair or not: everything happens based on causes and conditions, and the fact that we don't want to accept something doesn't stop it from happening.

Nothing lasts forever

We expect pleasant situations to last, objects to be reliable, relationships, social status and professional life to be stable, perennial and satisfying. We trust external things to give us stability and well-being, forgetting that nothing is permanent, solid or reliable. We then become deeply disillusioned with people and bitter about life when they don't live up to our expectations. It isn't the world's fault if we put too much trust in unreliable things, and then suffer when they let us down.

Life is only possible because change exists. If the heart didn't beat, if there were no inhaling and exhaling, if cells didn't renew themselves, we would not be alive. Even so-called inanimate matter is nothing more than a whirlwind of quantum particles in constant change: the solidity of the material world is, in fact, totally illusory. So how could we expect everything to stay the same day after day? Objects change, break, get scratched, stop working. We ourselves grow older by the minute and change our minds sometimes several times within an hour. So why are we so surprised when circumstances and people change? It's important to recognise that what we often call adversity is nothing more than the natural manifestation of change. But because we cherish the idea of permanence, change thwarts us, we resist it, making it more of a drama.

Reflection on impermanence plays a fundamental role in Buddhist training. Of course, everyone is aware that time passes and everything changes, but this is a reality that we prefer to forget. That is why we need to reflect on impermanence, contemplate on the innumerable, incessant changes so we can recognise in each one the natural manifestation of the flow of life. That way, we won't be so shocked when something changes in our lives.

You can use the meditation on impermanence at the end of this book as a way of familiarising yourself with the idea. Then in everyday life, whenever something changes, you can stop for a moment to contemplate that change.

Have realistic expectations

We are all steeped in the ignorance that makes us see the world in a false light. We are all controlled by negative emotions and we all put ourselves at the centre of our concerns. Since we have an ego, we all prioritise our own well-being above all else. Life can be difficult and we all have sufferings, traumas and challenges. We usually think it's legitimate to fight for our rights and safeguard our interests, and we don't even realise that by doing so we could be harming someone else. However, if someone does the same to us, we are outraged. We are quite blind to our own attitudes but hypersensitive to those of others.

If we look properly, we also change our minds, let friends down and can be ungrateful to those who have helped us, if it serves our purposes. To escape a difficult situation, we might condemn, slander or accuse others. When faced with certain behaviour, we may think: "How can someone act like that?" But if we pay attention, we may see ourselves doing the same thing.

Many of our disappointments are caused by the expectations we have of people. We think that parents, siblings or friends should have our well-being at heart, do everything they can to make us happy, be loyal and give up their interests in favour of ours. But do we do it for them? When we are disappointed by other's attitudes, we must think that we probably do or have done the same without realising it. We must remember that it is the nature of ignorance and suffering to act selfishly and unconsciously, and to direct our anger not at people but at the emotions that manipulate them—the same emotions that control us.

To say that we shouldn't expect too much from people sounds like the bitter conclusion of someone who has lost faith in humanity, but that's not what it's about. Because we are all self-centred, we can't assume others will behave in an altruistic and selfless way, because they most likely won't. In this way, we save ourselves a lot of grief and never become bitter, disappointed or unhappy. On the other hand, because not everyone acts selfishly or self-interestedly, we often get good surprises.

Don't assume bad intentions

When we get hurt by others, we often assume they have the worst intentions. In fact, altruism and respect for others are more common than malice and the gratuitous desire to do harm. Most of the time we commit negative actions out of ignorance and selfishness, blinded by suffering and lack of discernment. We are puppets in the hands of pride, envy, aversion and desire, and we are the first to suffer as a result. We try desperately, and unsuccessfully, to defend ourselves, protect our interests and improve our well-being, and the suffering we may cause others is nothing more than collateral damage, which we rarely recognise.

I'm not saying that deliberate, cold and calculating malice is impossible, but it is certainly much rarer than self-centredness. Persecuting someone takes work and energy, and people don't generally do it without ulterior motives, not just for the sake of being mean. If someone says something nasty, it is rare that it is really intended to hurt us, most of the time it's just because that person is in a bad mood, in pain or even inattentive. It is very rare that we were really targeted.

Not assuming bad intentions is actually the opposite of the previous point, not expecting too much from people. In both cases, it's important to understand what drives us, realising the power that fear, attachment, anger and all emotions have over us. In this way, we don't expect too much from our friends, nor do we imagine that everyone is trying to deceive and harm us.

We usually oscillate between these two equally unrealistic attitudes, which cause us a lot of suffering. The better we understand the difficult situation in which the ego puts us all, the better we will be able to develop a balanced and understanding attitude, accepting people as they are, with simplicity and openness but without taking unnecessary risks. The Dalai Lama expresses this contradiction with humour when he says: "We all have Buddha nature, but it is wiser to lock your door."

It's important to have enough discernment, understanding and compassion to be aware of how human minds work, knowing that aggressive and malicious behaviour can come from the people we least expect it from, but without this making us suspicious and bitter. Let's not assume bad intentions where we are not sure they exist and, if the facts prove that they do, let's try to understand the full extent of the suffering behind it. Everyone wins with that, especially us.

Stay in the present

We don't just suffer when something unpleasant happens; we also suffer through speculation, thinking that something bad is going to happen. We have a very fertile imagination when it comes to misfortunes, so we usually worry for no reason. If someone is late, it's much more likely that they've been held up in traffic than that they've had a serious accident. Just because someone doesn't answer their mobile phone doesn't mean that something bad has happened to them. We tend to imagine the worst and make a drama of any banal situation. The reality usually falls far short.

How often do we worry about things that never happen? If we hear about reorganisation in the company, we start to speculate. "Will they sack me? Am I going to change position? Will I earn less? How am I going to pay the mortgage?" And so on. We can spend a week drawing up black scenarios, losing our appetite and being unable to sleep, and in the end discover that it was about reorganising the office layout.

We constantly inflict unnecessary suffering on ourselves with this negative anticipation. Whenever I realise I'm dreading a hypothetical event, I think "I'm sure that if it happens, it won't be as bad as it seems. Whatever it is, we'll see when it comes!"

Sometimes negative anticipation conditions us to approach situations in the worst way and prevent them from going well. People with this tendency rarely realise that they are boycotting themselves, and the worst thing is that the more negative situations occur, the more they are sure that nothing works for them, so they approach every new situation with an increasingly negative anticipation.

An anecdote illustrates how we allow ourselves to be manipulated by negative anticipation. A man had been driving for many hours when he realised he had a puncture. He was in the middle of the countryside, tired and hungry; it was late at night and raining. Grumbling to himself, he got out of the car and opened the boot. But no matter how hard he looked, he couldn't find the jack to change the tyre. He remembered that his son had borrowed it and must have forgotten to put it back.

The man is furious. He thinks about calling the emergency services but has no phone signal. Out of his mind, he curses loudly and kicks the tyres. Not knowing what to do, he looks around and sees the faint light of a house in the distance. Realising that he can't stay in the middle of the road, he heads there, thinking that they might be able to help him.

Along the way, he gets angry at his son for being irresponsible; he blames his wife for spoiling their son; he gets angry at the rain; he complains about the tyres; he rebels against what he does; he hates the bad will of his customers. "It's just me! Alone in this wilderness! I wonder if there's anyone in that house. Maybe they won't even answer! Maybe they don't have a jack! Maybe they don't want to lend it to me!"

He reached the door of the house. In this state of irritation, he knocked violently on the door until he heard footsteps. "Who is it? What's going on?" asked a frightened voice from the other side. Seeing this as the confirmation of all his fears, he shouted "I knew you wouldn't even open the door! You can keep your jack, you bastard!"

Nothing is as good or as bad as it seems

When something good happens, we can feel ecstatic but when a difficulty arises, we can hit rock bottom. We tend to take everything very seriously and be either very happy or very apprehensive. The truth is, however, that things are never as good or as bad as they seem. All positive situations have drawbacks and all negative situations have qualities. What's more, an apparently negative situation can protect us from greater danger, while a positive situation can expose us to painful and unexpected consequences. It's not uncommon for people to win the lottery and ruin their lives because of it, just as it's not uncommon for accidents, illnesses, redundancies or separations to have unexpected and positive developments in our lives. Before we make our mind about something that happens, we should wait for what comes next. This story illustrates that wisdom.

A very poor widower had only two precious things in life: a son and a horse. When the horse disappeared one day, the villagers were very worried and came to see him. "Well, look at that! What bad luck! How will you manage without your horse! What a tragedy!" But the old man shrugged his shoulders, smiled and said "Let's wait and see. I'm sure we will manage."

After a day or two, the horse returned, bringing with it a wild mare. The people of the village got very excited. They came up to the old man and congratulated him, "You've been very lucky after all, we're very happy about what's happened to you! Now your life will change!" But the old man shrugged his shoulders, smiled and said "Let's wait and see. Who knows what else might happen?"

A few more days passed. While trying to tame the wild mare, his son fell and broke his leg. The people of the village were distraught. "And now what will become of you, without your son to help you? That was bad luck!" Again, the gentleman shrugged his shoulders, smiled and said "Let's wait and see. We will find a way!"

A few days later the boy was still in bed. The country went to war and the king's envoys came to recruit every able-bodied man in the village. All the boys left, except for the boy who had a broken leg. The people came back to the old man, "You have been so lucky! Your son didn't go to war he will always stay with you!" And he, as usual, shrugged his shoulders, smiled and said "Let's wait and see. Who knows what life has in store for us?"

This attitude is not indifferent resignation, but serene wisdom. It comes from observing the ups and downs of life and realising that nothing is as good or as bad as it seems at first glance. What's more, it is common for things to seem worse than they really are. With a little calmness and patience, we will see that over time things either get better or we learn to live with them. Sometimes it's enough to sleep on it so that the next day everything seems a little less bleak.

This too shall pass

Nothing in this world is permanent. All situations, no matter how terrible, have a limited duration. They can last for years, months or days, but eventually they pass, and sometimes unexpectedly. The world is always in a flux; there are millions of small and large changes taking place at every moment. Today's situation won't be the same tomorrow and tomorrow's situation will be different within a few days. Therefore, imagining that any situation, good or bad, will remain the same is just a fantasy.

We have all had moments in our lives when everything seemed lost, when we thought we'd never be happy again. Heartbreak, an economic crisis, a serious illness or the death of someone brings us to the brink of despair. But time passes, life goes on and we adapt. It's the natural cycle of life. "Nobody else will love me like this; I'll never be happy again; I'm never coming back..." These thoughts make us suffer unnecessarily. Nothing is definitive, nothing is guaranteed, everything changes. Life is constantly surprising us as we meet people we have not seen for years or return to places we had almost forgotten, when we least expect it.

There are times when we're doing well and times when we're doing badly, but both pass. In the course of our lives we've been in difficult situations that seemed to have no solution, we've felt that nothing made sense anymore, that we'd reached the end, and yet we are still here. That's why, when we're in a difficult situation, we should keep calm and think "Everything will pass and there's no point in anguishing over it. If everything works out tomorrow and

I haven't slept tonight, I'll have spent a sleepless night for no good reason".

I was told the story of a prisoner who was totally desperate, plunged into atrocious suffering. As he laid on the floor of his cell, he mechanically began to read the words and phrases that covered the walls. Among many obscenities, one phrase caught his attention: *This too shall pass*, and those words suddenly clicked. Every word on the walls had been written by someone. Someone who, like him, had sat in that cell, felt just as desperate and believed they had reached the end. And yet they had all gone their separate ways and now it was his turn. Apparently, this realisation completely changed not only that difficult moment, but his whole life.

One day at a time

Whenever we speculate about the duration of a situation, we create extra, totally unnecessary, suffering. In fact, the only thing we have to manage is this very instant, so duration is just a concept without any tangible, immediate reality. However, it is a concept that frightens and distresses us, much more than the actual suffering we are experiencing, here and now.

"Today was terrible and tomorrow will be worse. The day after tomorrow nothing will have changed and in six months I'll still be suffering. I'm doomed for the rest of my life." These thoughts don't refer to a specific pain or situation that is actually happening right now but are merely an assumption without any reality. Nevertheless, they deeply distress us.

Something I learnt at a difficult time in my life was that every day is a day and it's the only one we have to manage. Everything else is speculation. So, at the end of each day, instead of thinking, "It's been a terrible day and tomorrow will be worse!" I thought, "I made it to the end of the day. Tomorrow we'll see." I believe this is also a strategy used by drug addicts in the detox phase. At the end of each day, they look back and say, "I didn't do drugs today". They don't make promises or plans for the next day and don't burden themselves with long-term obligations. Each day is a victory or a defeat, but it's just one day. Tomorrow is a new challenge. Managing pain for a day is possible, but the thought of having to manage it for a month or a year terrifies us. We completely lose our strength and become so discouraged that we are unable to deal with the present moment. Thinking long-term in difficult times is overwhelming and depressing.

Guillaumet, Saint-Exupéry's pilot friend whom I've already spoken about, explained how he managed to walk for several days and nights in the snowy Andes where his plane crashed, "From the very first day, my greatest concern was to stop myself from thinking. The suffering was too intense and the situation too desperate. In order to find the courage to walk, I couldn't think about it. (...) What saved me was to take one step, then another and another. One step at a time." [9]

In difficult times, we must focus on managing the present moment. It would certainly be more comfortable if we did this at every

---

[9]Wind, Sand, and Stars, Saint-Exupéry.

moment of our lives, but when we face adversity, it's vital. Focusing only on the step we must take or the difficulty we must overcome makes them possible; predicting all the ones that will come next is unsustainable. When we manage one moment, one step at a time, we walk; when we imagine the journey, we fall, defeated and crushed by the weight.

We also must avoid comparing our current situation with a previous time when everything was going well, or with people who are doing well. It's natural to have these kinds of thoughts, but if we let them take hold, sadness, anger and other negative feelings will plague us. In normal life situations we can even slack off, but when we are experiencing a difficult situation, we can't afford to be inattentive. When we stop being aware, negative thoughts multiply and take root, making them much more difficult to eradicate. As soon as we notice them, we must intervene immediately.

At this point it is very important not to pass judgement or feel guilty. Take a deep breath, get in touch with the present moment and realise that dwelling on the past won't change anything. The previous situation is definitely over and nothing will bring it back. Life has changed so the best thing you can do is use your energy to work on the present. Strengthen your resolve, no doubt it will be difficult, but with practice everything can be achieved, and even more so when it's really necessary. Understand that you are trying to change a habit that makes you suffer for no benefit and realise that it's vital to avoid falling into negativity.

Improve what you can

A well-known Tibetan text says: "If something can be solved, you don't need to worry. If it can't, you don't need to worry either." When faced with a problem, we often ask ourselves a number of ancillary questions, such as who is to blame, how it happened or how it could have been avoided, instead of looking for a solution. When the situation is hopeless, it's pointless to continue speculating, moaning or accusing ourselves or others. Common sense recommends that we try to see if we can fix it and, if not, what we can do to make it better.

When the situation can be solved, there's no need to worry. All we have to do is find the best solution and put it into practice as quickly as possible. Choosing between several options can be tricky because there is not always one undeniably good one–everything has advantages and drawbacks. We should avoid actions that harm others, even if they immediately seem to solve the situation. We should also avoid quick fixes that have serious drawbacks in the long run and ponder the consequences of our choices. It happens often that in order to escape a difficult situation now, we get ourselves in worse problems later. I have seen how some of my friends, to escape very strict parents, ended up marrying the completely wrong person, or after a heartbreak hastily jumped into a new relationship. This often ends badly.

It also happens that we try so hard to find the right solution that we become paralysed with fear of making a mistake. Since we can't predict all the developments, it's impossible to know in advance what the results of each decision we make will be. However, experience has shown me that when we have good intentions and want to do our best, the result is generally good. The power of intention is such that even if we make a mistake, as long as we can maintain a positive attitude and accept the consequences, the end result can be very positive.

On the other hand, if we can't solve the situation, there is no need to worry either. Sometimes, we are so focused on radically and instantly changing the situation we find ourselves in, that we can't see the small adjustments that could bring us more comfort. Therefore, we always must evaluate what can be changed and what is unavoidable. In my example of the noisy neighbours, the inevitable part of the situation was that I couldn't stop them from making noise; the small adjustment that made all the difference was putting in earplugs. This distinction between what we have a solution for and what we must adapt to is fundamental so that we don't get stuck, suffering unnecessarily. Human beings have an amazing ability to adapt when necessary. If we don't block ourselves with opinions and pre-conceived ideas, we can adapt to the most difficult situations and quickly return to the level of happiness we had before.

If you find it difficult to adapt to a new situation, investigate where your resistance comes from. We often don't want to change habits that we identify with and that we feel are part of our *image*. For example, if we've got used to a certain standard of living–which identifies us with a social stratum–and we have to live more simply, we may feel that we've lost a part of ourselves. If we are forced to cut our budget and take public transport instead of driving our own car, we may suffer more from feeling embarrassed than from the inconvenience. Paradoxically, we often adapt more easily to practical inconveniences than to the feeling of our image being discredited. Almost every situation we face can be improved once we surrender to its obviousness. I've faced many changes, some quite radical and I've discovered through experience that it's possible to adapt and make life more comfortable even in situations that at first seem daunting.

Ultimately, it's basically about changing habits and the reason why this is so difficult is because they give us a sense of security. When our life is altered, we feel uprooted, vulnerable and lost, but it is only a matter of time before old habits are replaced by new ones.

We are not the thoughts

When we are tired, we tend to have negative thoughts. If we don't sleep well for a few nights and we're exhausted, we'll be more prone to thoughts of discouragement and sadness. If we give them too much importance and let them proliferate, we'll end up thinking we have problems, our life is terrible, we're very ill. The reality is much more prosaic, we just need to get a few hours of sleep.

As well as this, there are other situations in which physical reasons influence our state of mind. Liver disease or hormonal disturbances—the notorious premenstrual tension or the disturbances inherent in the menopause, for example—can be responsible for a more tense or emotional state of mind. If we don't understand where these disorders come from, we identify with our thoughts and manufacture problems for no good reason.

As we've already seen, we are not independent of our surroundings, which is why a bad diet, an unhealthy lifestyle or being in a demeaning environment (physically or emotionally) can have a negative influence on our moods. Understanding this helps to gain distance from what's going on in our heads. One of the results of meditation is that it allows us to observe instead of giving in to our thoughts.

If our state of mind is pessimistic, even the things that usually give us satisfaction become causes for discouragement. I've caught myself deploring situations that I really wanted and that others would have given anything to have! We must realise that not everything that comes to mind is justified and that we shouldn't feed the whims of our minds.

If we sleep badly and wake up in a bad mood, the simple fact that our coffee is cold or our bread is not toasted can be enough to start an argument. We leave the house in a bad mood and all that comes to mind are unpleasant thoughts: "I've got to get my car serviced; it's going to be difficult to park; I've got to put up with that insufferable customer; I'm fed up with the life I'm leading; nobody recognises my worth…" If we continue in this state of mind, as the hours go by, the problems and setbacks go on and we end the day frustrated. If many days like that follow one another, it will become a habit and a way of being.

Many of the enmities and conflicts, the biggest and most serious problems in our lives, almost all begin with a single thought. From the moment we look at someone and think "This person doesn't like me", we start interpreting negatively their behaviour and find reasons to hate them. This ill will shows through in our attitudes and words, the person feels it and soon what started out as just a bad feeling can turn into a real conflict.

When illness, the death of a loved one, a break-up or any other circumstance causes us to suffer, we should be careful not to let ourselves be overwhelmed by negative thoughts. We must not forget that we filter the world through our personal view and therefore what we see reflects who we are and what we constantly think about.

On the other hand, we should be aware that there is no rule, limit or logic to our thoughts and that they don't necessarily have any legitimacy or truth. We may not be able to control our thoughts, but we always have the freedom not to give them too much credit.

Don't hold grudges

Sometimes we can't forget the slightest humiliation or setback, even years and years later. We feel that by keeping that memory alive, we are somehow paying it back and fear to let it go and forget. The truth is that the resentment and hatred harboured towards the person who hurt us doesn't affect him in the slightest—it just poisons our own life for no good reason. Thinking about the wrong that has been done to us doesn't change the past, doesn't help in the present or predispose to happiness in the future. We sometimes have this absurd reaction as if, because we've had some difficulties, we need to throw everything away, sacrifice the happiness we can still share with others and become a victim forever.

If something has gone wrong or someone has betrayed us, harbouring resentment against life or the person is the best way to deprive ourselves of any well-being. The person who hurt us could never hurt us as badly as we hurt ourselves! Therefore, the best revenge we can take is not to dwell on it. Assuming that this person really wanted to make us suffer—which may not even be true—nothing can frustrate them more than if we don't let it happen.

Forgiveness is often seen as an act of altruism, but forgiving is necessary for our well-being and peace of mind. Until we forgive, we can't let go of resentment, we can't let go of the past and we needlessly prolong our suffering.

Avoid escalating aggression

In the event of a conflict, whether between people or countries, responding to violence with violence is never a good option. When we feel attacked, we tend to strike back, but paying back evil with evil leads to an escalation of harm that causes much more suffering for both sides. Instead of one aggression, we suffer several; instead of losing one thing, we lose many.

To justify retaliation, we say that we want the enemy to pay for what they've done. But to what extent does the suffering of others alleviate our own? Will it bring back what we've lost? All it does is to expose us to reprisals, further losses, and more suffering. If all we want is to alleviate our grief, why would we expose ourselves to worse suffering, even if, supposedly, it makes the enemy pay for what he has done? What's more, if we trust the law of causality, we know that he will suffer the consequences of his actions, and so will we. Therefore, there is no need for us to accumulate bad karma in order to make anyone pay for his acts for it will happen anyway.

In social or national conflicts, revenge is called for when people lose their lives. What is crazy is that the price to pay to avenge the death of one is often more deaths and more pain. Why would we be willing to do that in the name of so-called justice? In what way does it make sense to avenge the loss of one with the loss of many? We should bear in mind that there is no end to any conflict other than peaceful resolution; in the end, after much death and devastation, the two parties will have to sign the peace treaty. So why not do it as quickly as possible, avoiding suffering and saving lives?

To practise a conciliatory attitude, we must be at peace with ourselves. Those who have a guilty conscience are the first to vehemently defend themselves and strike back. If we feel confident about our actions and intentions, we can remain calm in the face of undeserved accusations and wait for time to prove our innocence. Even if that never happens, we will be at peace with our conscience and that is our most precious asset.

Having a conciliatory and non-violent attitude is not the same as turning the other cheek. When we are attacked, we must stop the person, if possible without resorting to violence or aggression. Retaliation is not so much an attempt to neutralise the enemy's attack as a desire to make them pay for their evil with greater evil. In this sense, while trying to stop others from harming us is a healthy and even altruistic attitude, wanting to make them pay is what fuels the escalation of violence, with devastating consequences for both sides.

We often think that, in order to impress others, we must demonstrate our strength through aggression, but some human beings find extraordinary and exemplary non-violent solutions.

The great Native American Indian Chief Sitting Bull taught the young people of his tribe an unforgettable lesson. Throughout his life, he tried to find a peaceful way to deal with the American government who systematically let him down. Because of that some considered him to be too weak. Towards the end of his life, as his authority began to wane, the great chief felt that, for the good of his people, he needed to re-impose himself as a charismatic leader. Then, during a battle against the American army, Sitting Bull performed an exceptional act of bravery. He got off his horse and, inviting anyone who wanted to join him, sat down between the two enemy lines to smoke a peace pipe. Of the handful of men who had the courage to follow him, eyewitnesses report that he showed no sign of anxiety. Strangely, none of those who sat with him were wounded. This extraordinary act of non-violent bravery had much more impact than if he had killed and scalped many enemies, something that any young warrior keen to show his mettle would more easily do.

Perhaps you think that only an exceptional being is capable of doing something similar. When we are fully aware of the pernicious and pointless nature of acts of violence and retaliation, and we have an upright attitude and the right motivation, similar solutions arise spontaneously in our minds. They may not be as remarkable, but they will be adapted to the situation we are in.

There are those who consider non-violence to be a manifestation of cowardice and weakness. But the bravery people show in violent situations is often false. Blinded by anger and hatred they become unaware of the danger and fearlessly attack a much stronger enemy. Opting for a non-violent solution is much more difficult and, because it is not a rushed act motivated by anger but a deliberate and wise decision, it requires greater courage. Throwing yourself at the enemy with hatred is certainly easier than getting off your horse and sitting down to smoke a pipe, as Sitting Bull did.

When we realise the devastating effects of aggressive retaliation, avoiding the escalation of violence is an act of wisdom that requires tolerance and courage in adversity. Even if it is more difficult to put into practice immediately, in the long run it saves us and others a lot of unnecessary suffering.

Dealing with anger

To prevent ourselves from escalating into violence, we must learn how to deal with anger. When we feel persecuted, victims of injustice, or the target of successive attacks, we feel anger and rage against those attacking us. The truth is that these feelings make us suffer much more than the attacks or injustices themselves.

If we look at the way our mind works, we'll see that the actual act doesn't makes us suffer as much as our reaction to it. For example, it's not usually someone's snoring that stops us from sleeping, but the irritation we feel. Similarly, it's not the act itself that gets on our nerves, but the fact that we see it as an injustice or an attack. An attack we don't recognise as such leaves us indifferent and, conversely, anything we assess as an attack will enrage us.

It's relatively rare for an isolated act to exasperate us, but when we've already considered someone as an enemy, even an irrelevant incident can infuriate us. Anger rarely comes cold, out of nowhere. Although it is an eruptive reaction that comes on suddenly, it is built up in time.

Strange as it may seem, dealing with anger and rage can be done in stages. When faced with an unpleasant situation, we feel annoyance. If we don't stop it immediately, it builds up to impatience, exasperation, and finally to a choleric outburst. All it takes then is the smallest spark to set off the explosion.

We might think that working through anger consists of containing it, i.e. being angry without showing it. However, the damage is just as terrible if it explodes as if it *implodes*. To deal with anger and frustration, we must recognise and defuse them before we get to that point. At the first signs of annoyance, we must try to dispel it before it gives way to impatience and exasperation; when we feel antipathy towards someone, we must prevent it from turning into dislike; and when we feel attacked, it is best to make ourselves clear.

When we are faced with difficult situations, we don't always manage to act calmly and thoughtfully. If we feel we are being targeted, it is difficult to calm down between two assaults and we might not be able to diffuse the tension. We must be particularly careful to avoid all occasions for conflict and take care to avoid speculation. Sometimes it's when we get home and can finally relax from the day's work and the conflict with a colleague, that we start thinking about the injustice of the situation, his dishonesty or arrogance.

We must realise which part of these feelings result from a mental construction that is built up in time. When a person's behaviour irritates us day after day, when we get angry in their presence and then in their absence, thinking about what they have done or said, we are preparing the ground for open conflict. It's therefore preferable to prevent things from getting to that point by not letting impatience take hold, and instead diffusing irritation, avoiding confrontation and not giving in to provocation. We must realise that giving in to anger, rage and resentment is like bringing home a serial killer, we'll never have a second's rest.

If you see that you are totally entangled in a conflict, that aversion and tension have already reached uncontrollable levels, running away might be the best thing to do. If you can avoid the person's presence and spend some time away from the conflict, it is a good idea to do so. Although the conflict will only be postponed, it may be useful to let things cool down and let your mind rest so that you can work with the exasperation better at a later stage.

Since a lot of our aversion is fuelled by the negative evaluation we have of the person, in order to diffuse the conflict, we need to transform it into something more positive. In Buddhism, we use the term *antidote* as a thought or concept that cancels out another and, in this case, if we understand that the aversion we feel was built up by accumulation, we can find positive aspects or qualities that counteract the negative ones. For example, we can try to find one positive point for every negative one. Although this may seem silly at first glance, it can be extremely effective.

If the conflict is very heated, we may not be able to find a single positive quality in our adversary. Not that they don't have any—everyone has good and bad qualities—it's just that our perspective is biased. If you are willing to do some inner work, you'll discover that it's your state of mind that determines how you see friends and enemies, and therefore it's from within that the solution to any conflict must come. If you think it might be effective, try the exercise I talked about in a previous chapter. Imagine your adversary in front of you and, as sincerely as possible, think:

Like me, this person just wants to be happy.
Like me, this person wants to avoid suffering.

Like me, this person has experienced sadness, loneliness and despair.
Like me, this person is looking to fulfil their needs.
Like this person I also sometimes make mistakes and sometimes do the right things.

If any of these thoughts seem easier to realise, start with it. For example, if you remember a time when that person went through a difficult phase in their life, it will be easier to think "Like me, this person has experienced sadness, loneliness and despair". Imagine how you would have felt in their shoes until a feeling of understanding and solidarity arises. When you feel that they are not that different from you or the people you care about, it will be easier to stop seeing them as a monster and recognise that they're just a person who, because they're unhappy, can't act in the best way.

This reflection will be easier the more accustomed we are to these exercises. That's why we always should train ourselves and not slack off when everything is calm and peaceful in our life. That way, when turbulence hits, it's much easier to have the right reflex. If we only remember to practise when we're already in an adverse situation, it will be difficult to start applying the methods at that time.

You're not the only one suffering

Suffering can make us focus more on ourselves than usual, making us think that our situation is more desperate than it really is. As terrible as it is, it's nothing compared to what it could be. As we've already seen, we tend to compare ourselves with those who are better off than us, or to remember good times when everything was going well, but we can't forget the people who are in worse situations than us, or other times when we weren't happy. If we don't close in on ourselves and listen to others, we'll realise that there are thousands of stories far more terrible than ours. We can be grateful for what we have, that our situation isn't as terrible as that of many other people.

An effective way to counteract this was given to me by a lady who came to one of my workshops. At the end she shared one of her tricks. She said that when she found herself asking the question "Why me?" she would immediately think: "Why not me?" By changing this question, we move from a heavy, self-centred attitude to a lighter more inclusive one. When we think "Why me?" it's like we feel we are somehow being targeted as if we are at the centre of the universe, whereas when we think "Why not me?" we are realising that there are countless people suffering and there is no reason why we should be spared. It seems like an obvious and simple thing, but it's very powerful.

Keep a sense of humour

The more we focus on ourselves and our problems, the more we think that they are serious, that we can't take them lightly, let alone with humour. Suffering then completely takes hold of our lives and the lives of those close to us. Aware of the seriousness of our situation, as soon as we have the opportunity, we tell others the endless list of our sorrows. Some people take everything very seriously, while others maintain a sense of humour in every situation. Being able to laugh at ourselves shows that we keep things light and can still find happiness despite everything.

A friend of mine, who died years ago, had an incredible sense of humour. He was not yet 30 when he was diagnosed with Parkinson's; he started out walking with a cane, moved on to crutches and finally a wheelchair. By his thirties he was totally dependent on others, but he never lost his sense of humour, his ability to laugh at himself. I remember having lunch with a group of friends and him complaining that he had nothing to occupy his time. We reminded him that it wasn't easy to give him a job. He immediately replied with a laugh: "Give me a whisk and I'll whip your egg whites!" Thanks to his sense of humour, he was always pleasant company and was never alone. And not just because he made us laugh: the truth is that his sense of humour kept him in a good mood and in a happy state of mind.

The difference between tragedy and comedy often lies in the way we look at situations. If you think about it, many situations that make us laugh could be seen as dramatic or catastrophic from a different point of view. That is why it is possible to choose to see events with humour.

Don't shut yourself in

When we suffer, we often seek solitude and isolate ourselves from others. This is not necessarily a negative thing. Sometimes we feel the need to be alone with the pain, in silence and without wasting energy on external things, in order to process it. Seeking internalisation and appreciating solitude are not necessarily synonymous with having closed ourselves off from others. But that's not always the case. Sometimes we distance ourselves from others to dwell on negative thoughts. We don't have the patience to listen to others, we don't want their pity and we can't bear to see them happy while we are suffering. We feel bitter about life and disillusioned, locked in a shell where no-one can get in.

Just as a toothache is all the more unbearable the more we focus on it, so psychological pain grows to disproportionate levels if we give it space. That is why when we're suffering, it's not a good idea to isolate ourselves and not want to see anyone. It's completely normal—and even healthy—to try to calm down and be alone for a few moments during the day, but that's different from shutting ourselves off from everyone.

It's not a good idea, for example, to stop working when we're going through a difficult situation, such as losing someone. While we're being urged on by the people and tasks around us, we don't have time to dwell on the situation. In the days following the loss of someone, the pain is usually too intense for us to deal with it face to face. At times like these, we must resist the temptation to isolate ourselves and try to fulfil our tasks and responsibilities instead. When the pain is less acute, we can then take some time to mourn and deal with our feelings.

When we close ourselves off from others, we become incapable of recognising the relative nature of our suffering. We're so immersed in our own thoughts that if someone reminds us that there are many people suffering, and some suffering much more than us, we get angry and say, "I don't care about the suffering of others!" We're blind to our surroundings and centred only on ourselves, endlessly reviewing all the reasons why what happened is unfair, shouldn't have happened and is the worst thing that has ever happened to anyone.

It is said that at the time of the Buddha, a village girl lost her little son. Devastated by grief, the poor girl wandered aimlessly through the fields and villages with her son's corpse in her arms, asking everyone she met if they could bring him back to life. No-one knew what to say, until someone suggested she go and see the Buddha, who was in a nearby village with his disciples. She did so.

When she found him, the girl begged him to bring her son back to life and, instead of giving her a discourse, the Buddha replied, "Yes, it's very easy. All you have to do is bring me a handful of sesame seeds given to you in a house where no one has died."

Ecstatic, the girl ran to the village and knocked on doors. Everyone, of course, offered to give her the sesame seeds, but when she asked if anyone had died in that house, the answer was: "Yes, last year, last month, last week, my father, my husband, my son…"

At first, she was so obsessed with her own pain that she didn't even listen to what people were saying, but after a while she began to listen. Some stories were so terrible that hers began to seem ordinary, not as dramatic as she had thought. She finally realised that death was universal, that no human being, no family could escape it. She felt less isolated and much closer to everyone. The barrier that kept her trapped in obsessive blindness fell away and she felt empathy and acceptance. She took her son to the cremation ground and returned to the Buddha, whom she thanked for his teaching and asked to accept her as a disciple.

Sometimes our blindness is such that we're not willing to listen to anything, not even from the person we respect the most. That's why the Buddha chose to confront her with reality in a direct way and not with words. So, in the worst moments of our lives, it's very important not to cloister ourselves in pain and anger, but instead to open ourselves up to the world and to others. Support groups, volunteering and all kinds of activities that force us to communicate, share and help are the best therapy.

Don't let suffering win

When we close ourselves off from grief, it's common to also distance ourselves from those closest to us. So, for example, it's not uncommon for a couple who lose a child to end up separating. While we can understand the reasons why this happens, we must recognise that it is completely absurd to add the pain of a divorce to the pain of a losing a child. These situations happen when we close ourselves off, becoming insensitive to the suffering of others, even the suffering of our nearest and dearest. So instead of gathering strength to face difficulties, we oppose and tear each other apart without any benefit to anyone.

If you have friendly and loving relationships with those around you, use them in difficult times so that you don't fall into an obsessive and closed attitude and, on the contrary, empathise with the pain of those facing the same difficulty. Instead of looking at them as enemies and shutting them out of your life, think about how they must be suffering and prioritise supporting them. Any difficulty in life is always easier to face if you have the support and warm presence of others.

Find an outlet

At difficult times in my life, I've discovered that it's important to find an outlet for the negative energy that dominates us. Intense physical activity, whether it's working out, doing sport or simply going for a walk, can help to release this energy in a healthy way, leaving us too exhausted to dwell on gloomy thoughts.

Many people immerse themselves in their work as a way of not thinking and keeping busy. It's a good strategy. However, if your professional activity is essentially intellectual, it would be a good idea to take up a sport, buy an indoor bike, start a regular exercise regime or deep clean a room in your house. You could take up voluntary work, go for long walks or do whatever it is that tires you out physically. Of course, this compulsive activity is an emergency measure, and it is neither necessary nor desirable to maintain this rhythm constantly. We can't escape the situation indefinitely. The day will come when we must face and transform this suffering. However, it might be easier once the suffering has cooled down a bit.

A useful and therapeutic way to put this advice into practice is to clean and tidy up your home or workplace. Put papers in order, catch up on administrative or financial matters, tidy up drawers, throw away anything that is damaged or no longer useful and, above all, anything that causes you negative feelings.

Communing with nature and the elements is also excellent therapy. Take a walk in the mountains; put your hands in the earth; dive into the river or the sea; let yourself be touched by the wind, the rain, warm yourself by the fire... Imagine that the complications and mental torture leave your body like a dark, sticky liquid that is absorbed into the earth, the water, the fire, the air... and recycled.

Animals are always excellent company, and even more so in difficult times. As they are close to nature and react instinctively, their presence is fresh and genuine, constantly bringing us back to the present moment. Although keeping a dog or cat in a city environment has a more complicated practical side, the fact that we have to look after them, walk them and give them affection connects us with the simple and healthy things in life. If you can't afford to have a pet, you can always volunteer in an animal shelter.

Writing, painting, singing, dancing or expressing what's in your soul in any form is another way of releasing and channelling contained energy. You don't have to be a great artist to express yourself. Arranging some flowers in a vase, setting a table with elegance, surrounding ourselves with beautiful objects are all examples of how your creativity can be expressed. Don't worry about the artistic value of your work—write, paint, sing, let your emotions come out! You may discover an unknown artistic vein, but the important thing is to release and transform the energy that causes you tension and pain.

How much music can you still play?

We tend to focus obsessively on problems and lose sight of the many things that are going well in our lives. The fact that you're struggling financially, for example, shouldn't stop us from appreciating the affection of our friends. On the contrary! We may have lost a child, but we have others who need our attention and care. If we've lost our sight, we still have four other senses that we can refine and develop. If we're paraplegic, we can still speak, listen, read, understand and, above all, love. It isn't that there is no pain in losing a child, going blind or becoming paraplegic–and I'm giving extreme examples here–but it's counterproductive to focus exclusively on what we've lost and forget everything we still have and everything we can still do with what we have left.

I heard this story, which I think illustrates, with elegance and grandeur, an attitude of courage in the face of adversity. Itzhak Perlman, the famous Israeli-American violinist, contracted polio as a child and wears a brace on each leg to enable him to move around. When he gives a concert, he has to make the journey slowly from backstage to the platform where he plays seated.

One day, Itzhak went to play a rather difficult piece at Lincoln Center in New York. During the concert, suddenly one of the strings on his violin broke with that characteristic sound that resembles a shotgun blast and which reverberated throughout the auditorium. The orchestra stopped immediately, and everyone waited to see what he was going to do. Instead of readjusting his apparatus, picking up his crutches and leaving the stage or waiting for a new string to be brought, Itzhak closed his eyes and concentrated for a moment. Then he signalled the conductor to continue and played the rest of the piece with the three remaining strings.

One person in the room recounted: "We all know that it's impossible to play a violin concerto with just three strings, but that night Itzhak Perlman pretended to ignore it. We could see him mentally rewriting the score as he played with breathtaking virtuosity. I think that at one point he even managed to extract an unprecedented sound from the strings of his violin. When he finished, the room was plunged into deep silence for a few seconds until people began to applaud in a crescendo of enthusiasm. Itzhak smiled, wiped his brow and raised his bow, asking for silence. Then, in a sweet and thoughtful tone without any kind of arrogance, he said: "You know, sometimes an artist has to find out how much music he can still play with what he has left!"

Don't turn adversity into an obstacle

Our greatest desire is to be happy and what we fear most is suffering. That's why, whenever something happens that goes against our wishes, we tend to overvalue it, thinking that happiness has become impossible. But, as we saw in the previous point, there are always positive aspects to any situation and it's up to us whether we turn adversity into an impediment or not.

Often, after a loss, an illness or a setback, we think that nothing good can ever happen again in our lives. We fixate on what makes us suffer, close ourselves off and block out any other feeling, especially if it's one of joy or happiness. We think that the situation is keeping us prisoner to the pain and we don't realise that we are the ones preventing ourselves from getting out of it. This process is quite paradoxical: on the one hand, because we want to be happy, we violently reject adversity; on the other, we get so caught up in rejection that we deny ourselves any chance of happiness. It's almost as if, every time some happiness emerges, we say: "I can't be happy because I'm suffering from not being happy!"

If we really want to be happy, then we must open up to happiness. Naturally, all beings want to feel good, to be at peace and in harmony. This aspiration is natural because it is an expression of the nature of our mind. On the other hand, unhappiness, anger and stress are altered, unnatural states. So why would we want to prolong pain any longer than is strictly unavoidable?

Even a serious accident or illness is not necessarily an obstacle to our well-being. When we are faced with something serious, we tend to think that the loss of a loved one, an illness or a serious disability will prevent us from ever being happy again. But the world is full of people with serious disabilities who, despite this, are happy and share their joy of life with others. The only true limitation and the only true freedom come from the mind, it is mind that can bind us and it is the mind that can set us free. Happiness and unhappiness are exclusively our own creations.

Whatever has happened, there is no reason why it should stop us from being happy again, able to give and receive love, feel joyful and fulfilled. What happened has caused us pain, but it's only natural that it will fade over time. The thing is, if we keep reactivating it—thinking over and over about what happened—it can go on for days, months and years.

Sometimes, in the middle of a crisis, we feel guilty if we find ourselves laughing. And we think: "How can I feel good, how can I smile, when this terrible thing has happened?" But life is just like that, a cycle of painful and happy moments in different proportions, depending on the circumstances. That's why it's very important to constantly remind ourselves that happiness is a choice whose impact doesn't just affect us. We may think that if we choose to be unhappy, it is no one else's business. But that's not true. If we choose to be unhappy and bitter, we will walk through life with a heavy brow, spreading unhappiness around us. We're all so interdependent that we can't be happy or unhappy on our own: we always drag others along with us. So even if we don't do it for ourselves, we should do it for those we care about, our children, parents, siblings and friends! Because they deserve to be happy.

Practical tips from chapter 5:

- Would you rather be right or at peace? Don't let matters of principle stop you from improving a difficult situation.
- Consider the fact that everything changes. Don't anticipate tomorrow because tomorrow doesn't exist—deal with one day at a time and think about managing only the present moment.
- Lower your expectations and don't presume bad intentions. Accept beings as they are.
- Choose non-violence and avoid retaliation.
- Change "Why me?" into "Why not me?"
- Laugh at yourself and remember that there is a fine line between comedy and tragedy.
- Recognise all the good you have left in life and cherish it.
- Get busy and find an outlet for negative energy.
- Be happy for others!

• CHAPTER 6 •

DEALING WITH PAIN

It may seem that pain, being essentially a physiological signal, is not likely to be affected by psychological factors. However, as set of sensations, pain inevitably depends on the mind and its evaluation. To that extent, everything we mentioned on how to deal with the aversion, anticipation and anguish triggered by any suffering equally applies to pain but it seemed useful to dig a bit deeper into the topic.

Pain is subjective

In the 17th century, René Descartes described pain as a biological response to a physical injury–a process like pulling a string to trigger a bell. In the following centuries, doctors continued to see pain as a sensation of strictly neurological origin. In this mechanistic approach, the intensity of pain is proportional to the severity of the injury, which means that two people with identical injuries feel the same degree of pain. In the last fifty years this view has changed radically, and scientists have begun to take a more holistic approach, realising that pain reflects the whole person. For pain to be felt it has to be interpreted by the brain. The brain combines the information from the body with emotions, beliefs, values, past experiences and cultural attitudes. Thus, the suffering experienced is not just neurological but the result of all these factors, and therefore pain is inevitably subjective.

The latest Positron Emission Tomography (PET) and functional Magnetic Resonance Imaging (fMRI) methods have allowed scientists for the first time to obtain images of the brain in real time, for example while someone is receiving a painful stimulus. This type of investigation has made it possible to conduct studies that reveal the full complexity of the phenomenon. One of them found that 64 per cent of the people studied had abnormalities in the intervertebral discs but did not complain of pain, while 85 per cent of the people who complained of pain had no detectable abnormalities.

One of the most widely accepted pain theories today is the gate theory, developed in the 1960s by Patrick Wall and Ronald Melzack. According to this theory, there are a kind of gates in the nerve connections, spinal cord and brain pain centres. In order to experience pain, the gates need to be open, which happens when there is an injury. The pain signals that we need to protect that part of the body and give it time to heal. When the healing process is complete, the gates close. What is interesting to note is that the process of opening and closing the gates is far from being simple and mechanical and seems to be affected by emotional states, mental activity and the way attention is directed. If the brain is expecting pain or is directed towards detecting it, the gates open and the sensation of pain is amplified. Thus, for people suffering from chronic pain, an unusual pain is felt to be much more intense for fear that it is caused by a new injury. Anxiety causes the gates to open or stay open for longer.

In this way, pain is never a purely physical sensation, it is always accompanied by emotion, so it is inevitably a psycho-physiological phenomenon. When we are talking about chronic pain, the apprehension caused by the expectation of pain becomes a fundamental aggravating factor, so that any attempt to manage pain must involve mental work to appease the mind.

The two arrows

In one of his teachings (*Sallatha Sutra*) the Buddha says, "When ordinary people feel pain, they worry, suffer and despair. They then feel two pains, one physical and the other mental. It's as if they were hit by one arrow, then another and they experience the pain of two arrows." This is what we feel when we experience physical suffering. In addition to the pain itself, rejection, fear and anguish generate within us a second type of suffering that adds to the first and is often greater than it.

The Buddha goes on "(People) resist and react against pain. This underlying feeling of aversion towards the painful sensation becomes an obsession." Thus, the reaction of wanting to ward off pain turns into aversion and this aversion quickly takes hold, causing much more suffering than the pain itself. When we feel overwhelmed by aversion and it becomes a habitual way of being, there is an intensification of negativity and there is no longer any room for well-being, happiness or any positive feelings or experiences. It's as if everything around us is painful, even what used to give us pleasure. We blind ourselves to beauty, affection and well-being and everything oppresses and torments us. This, of course, happens whether the first arrow is physical pain or any other kind of intense suffering.

But the Buddha continues "Faced with a painful sensation, ordinary people seek compulsive distraction. Why? Because it's the only way they know to escape it. This underlying tendency to seek distraction then becomes obsessive." When we try to escape the pain by distracting ourselves, we seem to erect a barrier between ourselves and the painful sensation, be it physical or mental. It seems like a logical reaction, and it can be, in occasional situations of acute pain, but if it becomes habitual, the result can be a worsening of the resistance and an increase of suffering.

When we look at our own experience, we can recognise our favourite escape habits, both in times of crisis and in general; eating, smoking, sleeping, watching TV, diverting our attention so that we don't have to deal with what we're feeling. It often seems to help, but the Buddha warns "By resisting and compulsively trying to distract themselves from pain, ordinary people are completely overwhelmed by it and sink into suffering and despair."

Experience shows that resistance, aversion and trying to escape pain–or any kind of suffering–aren't the best strategies even though they seem to be obvious. It is through them and the contradictory and conflicting feelings they generate that pain truly takes over our lives without leaving room for anything else.

In more common terminology, we speak of primary suffering–the first arrow - and secondary suffering–the second. The pain we feel is a fusion of both to such an extent that we often can't separate one from the other. However, this distinction is crucial because if we learn to separate the two types of suffering, we can reduce–or even eliminate–pain and anguish.

It's important to realise that, as unpleasant as pain can be, it's actually the secondary suffering that does the most damage. It drains us of all energy and enthusiasm and banishes all beauty and pleasure from life. When powerful emotions such as anxiety, fear or anger take hold, we become exhausted, weakened and tense, which has the effect of amplifying the pain in a downward spiral. It has now been proven that the intensity of pain increases when we feel anxious, tired or sad. These emotions act as amplifiers and open the gates of pain.

The effects of such emotions can be observed with a brain scanner. An Oxford University study, for example, shows the significant impact that even moderate levels of anxiety have on pain. In this study from the Department of Neurology, some anxiety was induced in a group of volunteers before touching the back of their left hand with a hot probe. The expectation of pain caused waves of emotion to travel through the volunteers' brains. It was almost as if the sensors of pain were turned up to the maximum to detect the slightest signal. In practice, what happened was that the *anxious* volunteers experienced much more pain than the *non-anxious* volunteers. And this additional pain showed up clearly on the scanner.

When people suffering from chronic pain fall into the vicious cycle of rejection and distraction described by Buddha, they begin to develop a state of chronic anxiety that amplifies all the signs of pain and turns their life into a hell.

The wise answer

On one hand, the secondary suffering arises as resistance, we try to run away from the unpleasant experience, and we feel agitated, restless and tense. We can't stop in one place, and we try to occupy ourselves with whatever distracts us from the pain. We think that these escapes provide us with the only moments of peace, and we enter a vicious cycle of addiction that generates more and more alienation, anxiety and panic. This attitude of rejection keeps us extremely tense, making us impatient, irritable and controlling.

At other times, we become obsessively dominated by pain. We completely lose perspective, and it seems that pain is the only reality, the only experience. We then become exhausted and it becomes difficult to do anything. At a certain point it may seem that the pain has taken over in a way that there is nothing left. We enter a state of apathy with lack of interest in everything. We tend to feel like victims and dramatise our situation, close ourselves off and can fall into depression.

In the *Sallatha Sutra*, after explaining how ordinary people react to pain, Buddha says: "When a wise person experiences a painful physical sensation, he doesn't worry, suffer or despair, and so he feels physical pain but no mental suffering. It's as if that person was hit by an arrow but there was no second one, so they only suffer the pain of one arrow. Thus, the sage is not afflicted by suffering and despair. This is the difference between him and ordinary people."

So whenever suffering or pain happens, instead of accepting the fact and taking the right and effective action to deal with it, we exhaust ourselves by fighting and burying our heads in the sand, creating, in the process, much more pain and anxiety.

When we live with chronic pain, the real problem is the tendency to be dominated by the negative side of things. Trapped in a vicious circle, we are so used to running away that we are rarely willing to reflect and end up suffering more from our idea of the situation than from the situation itself. But how do we break out of this hellish cycle?

The unlikely answer

Advances in medical science have provided us with new drugs to combat pain. Despite this, the most used substances are still opiates, such as morphine and oxycodone. These drugs can help a lot, but they also have many contraindications. On the one hand, they don't necessarily work 100 per cent—many patients continue to feel pain, albeit lessened—and, on the other, they create dependency and euphoric peaks. Plus, people often complain that these drugs leave them in a state of mental fog, unable to function normally.

As research into pain has progressed, conclusions about the subjective nature of the phenomenon have led some therapists to explore other, more holistic approaches that take into account everything we said about primary and secondary suffering. The impact that a change in emotions, ideas and values, as well as a clearer vision of the real situation, can have on the perception of pain has become evident. One of the essential tools for achieving this change was the introduction of meditation. Hundreds of studies on the effects of meditation carried out over the last few decades have shown the positive effects meditation has on attention, body awareness, depression, post-traumatic stress disorder (PTSD) and addiction. In these studies, meditation has also been shown to significantly reduce pain.

In a 2011 study at Wake Forest Medical Centre, Fadel Zeidan and his team studied a group of students and gave them a brain MRI while inducing pain. They were then asked to rate the intensity and discomfort of the pain. If the pain was music, intensity would be the volume while discomfort would be the level of emotion aroused. As expected, when the students felt pain, the area of their primary somatosensory cortex lit up. Over the next four days, the students learnt meditation techniques from a certified instructor for 20 minutes a day. On the fifth day, the researchers repeated the experiment. The results were very different. Activity in the primary somatosensory cortex had decreased to such an extent that it had become practically undetectable. But that wasn't all. Meditation had produced an increased activity in regions of the brain dedicated to emotion processing and cognitive control–areas where pain sensations are interpreted and constructed before they are consciously felt. It was interesting to note that the students more experienced in meditation had registered greater activity in these areas of the brain and, consequently, had felt even less pain than the others.

On average, the students experienced a 40 per cent reduction in pain intensity and a 57 per cent reduction in discomfort. But the most surprising and encouraging thing was the amount of practice needed to achieve this result: just four 20-minute training sessions! As for the more experienced, the results were even more spectacular, on average they experienced a 70 per cent reduction in pain intensity and a 93 per cent reduction in discomfort. Overall, the study concluded that the practice of meditation produced a greater reduction in pain than standard doses of morphine and other painkillers.

What Zeidan proved with his study is very important not only because it reveals the benefits of meditation, but also because it shows that these benefits can be achieved by mere beginners. Obviously, its effectiveness is proportional to the meditator's experience, but it's not necessary to have twenty years of practice to get some relief.

One of the reasons why meditation is so effective in blocking pain is that it doesn't just act on one level, but on multiple levels of pain processing. In fact, Zeidan and other researchers have recorded four areas of the brain involved in processing pain or regulating emotions and behaviour. These four areas are the primary somatosensory cortex, the anterior insula, the anterior cingulate cortex, and the prefrontal cortex, all of which show altered levels of activity during meditation.

The primary somatosensory cortex is the area of the brain directly responsible for processing pain. If a person cuts themselves, for example, it is this area of the brain that assesses the location and intensity of the pain of the cut. Next, the anterior insula, the area of the brain responsible for perceiving and regulating the body, recognises that there is pain and assesses its intensity. Then, the anterior cingulate cortex regulates the emotional response to the stimulus which leads to the person becoming angry or frightened at having cut themselves. Finally, the prefrontal cortex, the brain's command centre, generates the thoughts and actions appropriate to the information received, and inhibits those that are not appropriate.

Meditation alters the functioning of these four areas of the brain. By decreasing activity in the primary somatosensory cortex, the pain processing centre, and increasing activity in the other three areas, the intensity of the pain decreases. Taking the previous example: if the person who cut themselves was a meditator, Zeidan's studies showed that by decreasing activity in the pain processing centre the cut will hurt less. Then, by increasing activity in the areas of pain regulation and emotions, the person will tend not to evaluate the pain as being so strong and will adapt their behaviour and reaction accordingly.

Although meditation is not the only pain management strategy, it is a fundamental part. People who feel they have lost control of their lives and are trapped in a vicious cycle of suffering, need an approach that allows them to gain perspective. They need to separate the pain from the psychological suffering and observe each of them, calmly, without panic and without reacting. Meditative observation of sensations allows us to discover that pain is temporary and that it is not necessary to react to it so violently, paving the way for radical change. Meditative attention breaks down the idea we have about pain, allows us to face the monster, demystify it and learn to live with it. Over time, medication stops working and, if the psychological and social aspects of pain are ignored, there is no other strategy. Meditation, on the other hand, can treat pain on all levels, physical and mental, reduce anxiety and allow us to take back the reins of our lives.

Meditation for pain management

It was through someone I met at one of my lectures in UK that I heard about Vidyamala Burch. This lady had a spinal injury at the age of 17, two surgeries after a car accident and has lived with chronic pain and partial paraplegia for over 20 years. Her journey led her to learn Buddhist meditation and to train with Dr Jon Kabat-Zin, the *Mindfulness for Stress Reduction* (MBSR) programme. As a result of this training and her personal experience in pain management, Vidyamala developed a set of techniques and strategies, based on meditation, to enable patients with chronic pain, disabling illnesses or any other form of chronic stress to live better lives. She added a lot of research to her personal experience and began to teach these techniques, giving them the name MBPM (*mindfulness-based pain and illness management*), a wise management of pain and illness based on mindfulness meditation. In 2004 Vidyamala founded an organisation based in UK she called Breathworks. They train accredited instructors and there are many available courses in different locations and online.[10]

What is Mindfulness? This meditation technique is no different from basic Buddhist meditation in terms of paying attention to

---

[10] Check their website at https://www.breathworks-mindfulness.org.uk

breathing, sensations and, in general, the present moment. For convenience, it avoids any association with a spiritual tradition and is only considered as a technique for developing attention which can be used in clinical, business or other contexts without hurting any convictions or sensitivities.

What we are talking here is a kind of spacious attention in which we are fully aware of the moment, but in a non-controlling way and without evaluation or judgement. Instead of being caught by or sucked into thoughts, we look at them with full awareness. If we look at our experience in this way, we'll conclude that only the experience of *now* has any reality. The sensation we are feeling, the sound we are hearing, are our experience. Any memory of past, or speculation about future experiences, only exists as a mental construct.

Developing this type of awareness allows us to realise that all experiences are transitory, and we can be more aware of them than caught in the concept we have of them. There is usually a big difference between the experience of something and its mental representation. Being aware of this difference allows us to deal with the actual experiences and avoid being overwhelmed by the ideas we have about them. This awareness of thoughts, emotions, and physical sensations as they are experienced in the present moment helps us move from reactive, automatic behaviour to an attitude where there is initiative and choice. Mindfulness meditation creates a sense of space in which we can explore sensations, including those of pain, and observe them as they are, thus paving the way towards acceptance.

As we've seen, secondary suffering can be seen as resistance to pain. Since none of us wants to suffer, it's perfectly natural to fight it and resist it with all our might. We want to do anything to get rid of it. It's understandable but, as we've seen, it's also the wrong approach because it creates much more pain. But while resisting the pain can make it worse, acceptance can reduce and even eliminate pain altogether. It sounds absurd, but neuroscientists say that "what we resist persists". In other words, when we resist the body's messages, those messages continue to be sent until we accept them. As soon as we consciously accept and feel them, they have done their job and tend to disappear of their own accord.

It's common for acceptance to be misunderstood and even negatively seen by people facing chronic pain. It's important to realise that conscious acceptance is not resignation, but the assessment of the situation as it is, at least for the time being. And this is fundamental if we are to begin the process of pacifying suffering.

It is possible to explain how this happens in theory, to study the numerous scientific studies that prove it and even to see scans of the brain, but only when you've experienced the power of awareness will you believe it. And what do you have to lose? Accepting pain can be very difficult, but it's better than the alternative: living in a state of perpetual suffering.

Five phases of mindfulness

Breathworks courses guide participants through meditation in five steps. Here I'll explain each of them, but at the end of the book you'll find the corresponding meditation exercise. Of course, it's preferable to attend a course in person, go on a retreat or follow the instructions of an accredited teacher. But for those who can't, I'll try to share the information you need to do it yourself. Perhaps you think you're so trapped in the vicious circle of negativity that you can't get out on your own. However, all human beings have resources that they only use when they are desperate. One of the great wonders of life is that extreme difficulties, when accepted with awareness and openness, bring out the best in us. If you think you've hit rock bottom, know that the time has come, this is the turning point! And meditation can be exactly the tool you need to take a new direction.

It all starts with full awareness. It's nothing mysterious in itself; on the contrary, it's the simplest and most natural thing in life, the simple fact of being present in what we're doing. Although simple, it may not be obvious because we are always much more involved with our inner discourses about things than with the things themselves. This discursive thinking can be seen as a kind of voice-over. Eckhart Tolle talks about "a voice in the head". This internal discourse creates a separation between us and the experiences and almost completely captures our attention, so that we are often walking around, immersed in our thoughts and oblivious to what is really going on. That's why we don't know where we've put the keys or if we've taken our tablets.

Mindfulness meditation brings us back to the moment, to the concrete reality of our experience. We gain awareness of obvious things like breathing, listening, feeling, sitting or walking. It allows us to notice everything, without judgement, without comment. It even allows us, over time, to observe our own thoughts and emotions from the outside, without being sucked into them and seeing the world through their eyes.

Withdrawing our awareness from thought and placing it on something that is part of the experience of the moment, such as breathing, sensations or sounds, is like stepping out of a river, where the strong current is dragging us along uncontrollably, and sitting down on the bank. The river continues to flow, but now we have stepped back to peacefully observe it. And whether beautiful or ugly, frightening or fascinating, everything passes. It's very simple and natural, but as it's not the kind of awareness we usually have, we need to train ourselves. Meditation is that training.

As this type of awareness develops, we'll be able to better observe all experiences. If we are aware of a sound, we can hear it as such and not as a designated noise. This means stripping it of any label and of any pleasant or unpleasant connotations, so that all we hear is a sound, like if we were a baby hearing it for the first time. When we apply this cognitive *striptease* to any experience, we see how much lighter it feels. In the context of pain, this is precious and paves the way to the next step.

We could describe it as "exploring discomfort" and it's completely counterintuitive. As we've seen, the usual reaction to pain being rejection, focusing on it is the last thing we want to do. We think that if we pay attention to the pain, it will hurt more. However, looking at pain in the way we've described allow us to demystify it and realise that it's not a thing but a process. One of the participants in the Breathworks course says: "I had never really looked at pain and had turned it into a monster. I tried to look at it. What was its shape? Where was it located? What colour was it? I tried to find out the true nature of pain and discovered that I had solidified it and that it was actually an experience that changed from moment to moment. When I noticed these fluctuations, I was able to feel the pain instead of being overwhelmed by my reactions."

It's possible–and even likely–that the pain is initially hidden behind our resistance and aversion to it. If this is the case, we should observe them and open ourselves up to them, sit on the riverbank and, with kindness, look at all the tension gathered around the unpleasant sensations. Approaching our rejection with kindness will allow us to loosen the knot, relax and gradually be able to explore the underlying painful sensations.

Through this exploration we will discover all its modulations. Pain is not a solid thing like a rock in the middle of a river. It is a flow of sensations with moments of normality and peaks of pain. We may discover different sensations such as heat, cold, constriction, throbbing and realise that not all of them are completely unpleasant. The different sensations come and go like waves; they constantly change in character and intensity. As we explore each one of them, moment by moment, we may end up accepting that they are like logs being dragged by the current of the river: we see them approach, stay for a moment and then disappear.

At this stage we start noticing a spacious feeling that comes from having stepped out of our sensations and placed ourselves as observers. We see that our mind can be compared to the sky and our sensations, thoughts and emotions to the clouds. Mindfulness meditation allows us to observe this process without getting caught in it and to discover that, whatever happens, the sky–our mind–remains untouched. As Pema Chodron says: "We are the sky, everything else is the weather".

As in the example of sound, thanks to this investigation, pain will lose its density. By stripping it of preconceived ideas, we begin to see it as it is and recognise that this flow of sensations, whether neutral, pleasant or unpleasant, is the flow of life. Strangely enough, only when we have the courage to look at our pain can we begin to free ourselves from it.

The third step is, in a way, even more unexpected because it consists of becoming sensitive to the pleasant aspects of our experience. Living with pain tends to trap us in a state of resistance and aversion in which we block the pain out and try to distract ourselves from it with all kinds of addictions. We may even be able to ignore it for a while but all to the detriment of the rest of our life. Our world becomes grey; food loses its taste and texture; we've stopped laughing and crying. So, asking us to focus on the pleasant aspects of our experience seems ridiculous.

Even if it seems impossible now, by travelling this path of pacification in relation to the pain, everyone can find something positive, pleasant or even beautiful in their experience, if they know how to look for it. It can be simple things like the warmth of a hand, the feel of a clean sheet, the comfort of pillows, a ray of sunshine coming through the window, the scent of a flower... We need to let go of the ideas about our situation and approach this experience with an open mind. After all, what have we got to lose?

Strange as it may seem, this third step arises naturally as a consequence of the second: once we have experienced pain as a stream of unpleasant sensations, we will be led to discover that there are others. This conscious exploration of sensations leads us to discover a wide variety of emotions such as rejection, sadness, discouragement, but also happiness, love, compassion and empathy. We discover that life is bittersweet and that this is the reality of our human condition, whether we live with pain or not. This realisation makes us more open and empathetic, sensitive to the world outside.

At this stage we are ready to tackle the fourth step. Mindfulness meditation expands as if it has become a container big enough to hold both pleasant and unpleasant sensations. If our attention was a camera lens, in the previous two steps it would have been a macro lens, capable of focusing at a very short distance and capturing the tiniest details. Now we're moving away and switching to a wide-angle lens.

The more stressed we are, the more we feel like we don't have room to contain everything that's happening, as if all the experiences are squeezed inside us. When we feel like a big container, awareness of the moment expands in such a way that sensations, thoughts or emotions are nothing more than small events within that vast expanse. We are aware of everything that is happening, but without losing perspective. Accepting the totality of the experience brings great relief and allows us to relax more completely. Naturally, a feeling of connectedness emerges from this space and we begin to enjoy the presence of others.

The fifth step introduces the freedom to choose to respond rather than react to experiences, especially unpleasant ones. Of course, we have already chosen to be aware of our experience rather than avoiding it, to open up to the unpleasant sensations and expand our awareness. In all the previous steps we have chosen awareness rather than alienation and this has enabled us to distinguish between the two types of suffering and dissolve the monster of pain. So, instead of feeling that pain controls us and that we are its powerless victims, we realise we have the freedom to find creative solutions when faced with life's situations, even the most painful or radical ones.

What's the difference between responding and reacting? The more aware we are of the situation and accept it for what it really is, the more able we are to act appropriately and realistically. So, for example, if we accept that we have an injury that causes pain if we sit for more than thirty minutes, we know that we have to lie down every half hour and take advantage of that time to do a few minutes of conscious breathing. This is responding.

But if, instead, we feel frustrated at not being able to do what we used to do or what others do, with some anger we may unnecessarily prolong the effort just to feel normal, to prove to ourselves that we can do it or any other reason that stems from an emotional reaction. This is reacting.

The results are very different in either case. While the first approach has a chance of allowing us to lead a balanced and, over time, practically normal life, the second makes us constantly oscillate between good and bad days, between hope and despair.

This meditation-guided approach is a kind and understanding technique for our body and mind. There's nothing complacent or pious about it, it doesn't come from a feeling of victimhood. It's a total acceptance and de-dramatisation of our situation. We are no less than anyone else, we are not a victim of anything, we just have some limitations that we need to learn how to manage.

TSERING PALDRON

Wise pain management

Mindfulness meditation and its capacity for enquiry leads to a realistic recognition of the situation we're in, stripping it of preconceived ideas and reactivity. We are thus much better able to deal with reality and manage our situation wisely. In a way, this presupposes letting go of the fight against pain. But we must be careful not to misunderstand what this acceptance means. It is not resignation in the sense of giving up hope of a cure or abandoning therapies. Accepting the situation as it is means that we are aware of our limitations but we don't necessarily withdraw from all activity. We have a realistic approach towards our condition but we don't give up all hope of recovery. We don't live in constant *disagreement* but adapt our actions to achieve symptomatic relief and the best possible quality of life.

And in this sense, it's very important to clarify the issue of medication. As it was mentioned in the conclusions of Zeidan's study that meditation produced more pain relief than narcotics, you may have got the impression that the idea is to do without medication. Although this may be the case, the two approaches don't have to exclude each other. People often fear that antidepressants or narcotics are incompatible with meditation because they cloud the mind. But doesn't pain also cloud the mind? We must be sensible and realise that the best approach is to find the right dose of medication to enable us to take all the other actions that bring comfort, perspective and quality of life.

Thinking something like "I should be able to bear the pain" or "It's not right to take so much medication" are reactions, not responses. Medication isn't *evil* and meditation isn't *good*, it's not a fight between what's right and what's wrong. Meditation allows us to choose the most realistic approach and find balance, taking enough medication to function with as much mental clarity as possible depending on the intensity of the pain.

Sometimes the pain can be so intense that it's simply impossible to meditate. It's very important not to have the feeling that we've failed because we should be able to meditate despite everything. If it's a temporary condition, we can do our best and hope it goes away, but if it lasts, we may have to review our strategies and consult our doctor to readjust the medication. Throughout this process it is very important to feel that we are being followed and supported by health professionals, be they doctors, physiotherapists, psychologists or others and also, if we want to try the path of mindfulness, by instructors who can guide us. Support groups work very well because they allow us to share experiences and tips as well as putting complaints into perspective. All of these advantages presuppose that we live in a place where we have access to this type of care and where we can find counselling and support groups. I hope this is the case for you, as it makes it easier. But if not, don't despair!

Nowadays in Western Europe, everyone has access to healthcare, so you should seek help to find the right medication and consult your doctor whenever you feel we need an adjustment. With regard to meditation, you should try to find someone who can guide you through the various steps of mindfulness, but if not, you can follow the instructions at the end of the book. To make the practice easier, you can download an audio file of the guided meditation on my website so that all you have to do is save them onto an mp3 player or a mobile phone, put some headphones in your ears and follow the instructions. Alternatively, you can record the instructions in your own voice and use that audio in the same way.

As for support groups, if there aren't any in your area, look online. Nowadays, social networks and other digital tools allow people who are more isolated to find each other. Alternatively, look at starting a group in your area.

Meditation on pain is not a different type of meditation and, therefore, all the investigation processes described in here can be applied to any other object, whether the sounds, the breathing, thoughts or even the nature of the observer itself. However, it seemed useful to write about it in a more specific way because our intense aversion to pain doesn't predispose us to investigate it.

Living with pain or any other limitation doesn't have to be hell. There are countless examples of people who have learnt to manage their illness, disability and pain in such a way as to not only maintain an active, useful and meaningful life, but also to be happy and enjoy beauty and love. As we learn to appreciate the richness and depth of the present moment, we open our hearts and become more intensely alive. It then becomes possible to joyfully take everything in our stride.

Practical tips from chapter 6:

- Pain is a subjective phenomenon that depends on the person as a whole.
- The mindfulness approach can change every aspect of your experience by acting on four pain-processing brain areas.
- Train in mindfulness.
- Explore the discomfort.
- Open yourself to pleasant sensations.
- Discover the inner space—accept the totality of the experience.
- Respond instead of reacting.
- Manage yourself wisely to achieve the best possible quality of life.
- Mindfulness should extend to your whole life.

• CHAPTER 7 •

SUFFERING AND THE SPIRITUAL PATH

From the fundamental Buddhist point of view, suffering is not inherent to our nature, nor is it necessary. Suffering happens as a result of causes, as Buddha explained in his first teaching. So, it is not like we are *meant* to suffer because it is the nature of our mind to be miserable. On the contrary, when our mind is left in its natural state, we experience joy, peace and love. Suffering is an altered state.

Now of course, for us unenlightened beings, suffering is inevitable. Unless and until we have exhausted what causes it, we can't expect to enjoy perfect happiness. Not only that, but we all can recognise the important role of suffering in making us more mature and empathic as human beings. This is probably why all the world's spiritual and humanist traditions, have valued suffering as something that is not only inevitable, but essential on a spiritual path.

I'm not talking about a morbid pursuit of suffering as atonement for sins or *mortification of the flesh;* these are unhealthy misrepresentations of an authentic and powerful spiritual message. It isn't about inflicting ourselves pain as punishment for something we've done or even for the ancestral sin of not having resisted the apple. However, if we read the stories of the great thinkers, reformers, visionaries, artists or saints of all time, we will see that they all faced hardships and that it was these that largely contributed to making them exceptional beings.

When everything goes our way, we let ourselves live. Even when a passing setback prevents us from achieving what we want or confronts us with what we seek to avoid, escape and distraction are our favourite strategies. If we don't have to, we are never willing to take a closer, more investigative look at the world and ourselves. We find it more comfortable to live in this semi-conscious slumber and we don't want to be woken up.

We've already seen that the Buddha called this lethargy *avidhya,* unawareness. The word Buddha means "awakened", someone who has awakened to an awareness of reality. Curiously, most of us only wish to awaken when they are faced with suffering. Buddha seems to be an exception because, as far as we can tell from his story, his situation was very favourable. As a prince, he enjoyed every comfort and lacked nothing. However, he left the royal palace and renounced the throne because he realised the suffering of others and wanted to find an answer to it. So, deep down, suffering was also the driving force behind his awakening.

When we're faced with adversity and can't distract ourselves from it, we're forced to wake up to reality. It's like an alarm clock that goes off when we're in our deepest sleep. Suffering shatters illusions and breaks our fascination for sensory pleasures. It confronts us with impermanence and reveals that the material world isn't as reliable or secure as we imagined, urging us to look for something else. If we look at it from a spiritual point of view, suffering is a great ally. It pushes us to overcome limitations, preconceived ideas and spiritual lethargy and to discover the treasure that lies behind them. So, this is why we might say that suffering is necessary… until it is no more.

Why do we suffer?

In this state of unawareness, it's easy to be confused. Not only do we deceive ourselves about the nature of phenomena, but also - and above all—we are ignorant of our own nature. It was this realisation that prompted the motto "Know Thyself" inscribed on the temple of Apollo in Delphi. It's not so much about knowing our qualities and defects or undergoing psychotherapy as it is about deeply investigating the nature of our consciousness. After all, who or what are we?

Our mind experiences all kinds of sensations, perceptions, thoughts and emotions that constantly follow one another. In general, we feel that there is experience and *experiencer*, someone to whom that experience belongs and with whom we identify when we say *I*. In his book *A New Earth*, Eckhart Tolle says the following: "Most people are so completely identified with the voice in their head—the incessant stream of involuntary and compulsive thinking and the emotions that accompany it—that we can describe them as being possessed by their mind. As long as you are completely unaware of this, you take the thinker to be who you are. This is the egoic mind. We call it egoic because there is a sense of self, of I (ego), in every thought—every memory, every interpretation, opinion, viewpoint, reaction, emotion. This is unconsciousness, spiritually speaking."

Of course, it's not the experience sensations, thoughts and emotions—that's at stake. It is undeniable. What is at issue is the distinction we make within it, creating an artificial *I* with which we identify and which we conceptualise as the *experiencer* or the *thinker*. That is what contaminates our entire experience of the world.

Eckhart Tolle goes on to say: "When you live through the mind-made self comprised of thought and emotion that is the ego, the basis of your identity is precarious because thought and emotion are by their very nature ephemeral, fleeting. So every ego is continuously struggling for survival, trying to protect and enlarge itself."

This precariousness of the ego gives us a permanent feeling of insecurity and restlessness, a constant desire to assert and reinforce ourselves, either through material things—everything we can possess—or through others. It is this craving that Buddha called *dukkha,* usually translated as suffering, but which in fact means dissatisfaction—as we already said.

If all this is completely new to you, it probably doesn't make much sense. You may understand it intellectually, but it might not resonate within yourself. On the other hand, when we have some experience of meditation, we may have already experienced brief moments in which the observer faded a little, or even disappeared, leaving only the experience. To describe this, a Zen master could say something like: "It is like sound hearing itself".

Ringu Tulku Rinpoche, in his book *Mind Training,* says: "We have created the illusion of a unique and unchanging self, an individual "I" that we believe remains fixed somewhere within us all the time as feelings and thoughts come and go. In Buddhism the term we use to describe this is "ego." Our assumed identity leads to discrimination and splits the natural oneness of our mind into two. It imposes a dualistic relationship between our ego-self and the object, dividing experience into sight and the seer, feeling and the feeler, or thought and the thinker. This is the basis for our grasping. "Wanting this" and "not wanting that", we project the attachment and aversion of the ego onto the external world. In fact, there is no "I" beyond our basic consciousness, no "I" different from the experience. We do not have any ownership over it. If we do not recognise this and subdue these projections, we will continue to suffer."

This investigation is essential because, without it, we will continue to blame situations or others for our suffering and–more importantly–each time we do so, we cannot put an end to it.

The ego's shell

Due to a lack of investigation, we allow the sense of identity to solidify, and everything we experience and do is constantly reinforcing it. It's like a permanent state of alert in which we are never relaxed. Whatever happens is immediately evaluated: is it a threat, a reinforcement or a neutral situation? What do we have to lose? What do we have to gain? The more intense our sense of identity, the greater the unease.

In order to feel more protected, we build a shell around ourselves. This shell–which sometimes looks more like a wall–is essentially made up of fear: fear of being weak; fear of suffering; fear of exposing oneself; fear of losing, and above all, fear of not being recognised or of disappearing. The more fearful we are, the more our ego compensates with arrogant, aggressive, insensitive and controlling behaviour. The more it wants to be right and set itself apart from others–in a positive or negative way–the more it is imbued with ideas and concepts about everything. The more fearful the ego is the more it reinforces its shell with successive layers, to the point where it seems to be completely blind, deaf and insensitive to others.

That shell rejects the suffering of others, under the most varied pretexts. It can claim, for example, that certain human beings don't have souls or that animals don't feel pain; that the drunk who fell in the street gets what he deserves and many other arguments on which other people's pain slides off. To a certain extent, this shell actually works. Shielded behind our indifference, we manage not to be affected by anything as long as it doesn't touch us directly. If the upstairs neighbour suffers in silence, no one cares, but if he spends the night shouting, everyone will be keen on finding a solution. Not necessarily to end his suffering, but at least to end the shouting.

It's because of this shell that it's always the other person's fault, that we are always right and that, when we can't avoid someone else's suffering, we touch them with the non-stick gloves of pity – "Poor guy's having a hard time, but better him than me!" It's because of this shell that the past and the future are more important than the present and it's also what keeps us absorbed in the world of our mind and totally alienated from reality. Because of it, we go through life on autopilot, numbed, insensitive to the suffering of others–perhaps–but also to everything else.

When the shell is intact, life's little pleasures have no appeal. Happiness can only be found in a faraway place, in an inaccessible love, in a dream holiday–in something sophisticated and valuable other than the present. In fact, as soon as these things are no longer inaccessible and do happen, they become the present and lose their charm.

When the shell breaks

All it takes is for something or someone to thwart us for the shell to be scratched and the ego to go into restoration mode. If it were a colony of ants, we'd see them rushing to the scene of the accident to fill in the scratch and polish the shell until it is fully restored. That's why we don't leave an argument without being proved right or, if we can't, at least without having shaken off our responsibility onto someone else. Restoration strategies include everything the ego uses to refurbish itself, from buying a pair of shoes or a mobile phone, to eating chocolate or drinking a glass of wine. Restoration allows the ego to recover from minor accidents, but it is also a daily and habitual compensation strategy. Many of our habits are ways of pampering and restoring the ego.

A bigger jolt, a violent argument or a more serious threat triggers the survival mode. That's when the ego completely loses its mind. In a heated argument, we often hear people say things that are illogical, totally unreasonable and completely incoherent. In survival mode, the ego panics and fires blindly. When we are in this mode, we are unable to listen to reason and are therefore completely impervious to the best and most sensible arguments. In these conditions, any exchange of words is completely pointless and only serves to inflame tempers further.

However, if the blow is violent, the previous strategies no longer work. It's no longer just a scratch or dent in the shell: a vital threat is a breach that is impossible to ignore and the shock can be so great and so sudden that we are left without reaction, disorientated. Such a shock breaks our shell, leaving the inside completely exposed. And the thicker the shell, the more fragile the inside and the greater the panic.

Once the paralysis has passed, the ego tries to rebuild itself. Depending on the nature and intensity of the blow, there may be various types of strategies to re-establish the integrity of the shell. Rejection of the situation, anger, the need to find culprits and other reactions of aversion are all replacement strategies. Unfortunately, if we are dealing with painful and irreversible situations, none of these strategies will protect us from whatever is causing the suffering and, on the contrary, all of them will only exacerbate it. In an attempt to rebuild the shell, the ego focuses completely on itself, becomes aggressive and intolerant, even more indifferent to others than usual. The fact that it is focused on itself accentuates the feeling of separation and it suffers horribly from being a victim, handpicked and completely unfairly chosen to live in that situation. All these reactions thicken the shell. The ego is strengthened both positively and negatively, which is why a traumatised ego is more self-centred than a balanced one.

Due to habit and social and cultural conditioning, we often react in this way to suffering and, as a result, aggravate our suffering and thicken our ego with every difficult situation that life throws at us.

The loss

I used to think that suffering was like a magic wand that had the power to sweep away self-centredness and make way for compassion and empathy. I thought that we inevitably came out of difficult situations better people, more sensitive and compassionate. Unfortunately, the opposite is also true. Experience has shown me that it's not suffering that changes us, but how we accept it. Acceptance is totally counter-intuitive for the ego because it means giving up replacement strategies and becoming vulnerable. For the ego, acceptance is death. And indeed, it is.

All major changes, bereavements or losses are experienced by the ego as death, partial or complete, depending on the case. It feels deprived of a part of itself, as if a limb had been taken. In fact, since it identifies with opinions, relationships, status, possessions and virtually everything it appropriates, any loss is a threat.

Thus, the psychological process of mourning described by Elizabeth Kübler-Ross with its five phases of denial, anger, negotiation, depression and acceptance, although it was developed by observing the reactions of terminally ill patients, is applicable to all major changes or losses in our lives. Depending on the person, these phases can occur in a different order or not at all.

When we are confronted with something that deeply shakes us, we go into denial. At this stage we say, "This can't be happening", or "I want to wake up and find out it was just a bad dream". We're convinced that the diagnosis is incorrect, that the letter came to the wrong address, that the person will change their mind, that it's a bad joke. We have a feeling of unreality, as if everything has lost its meaning. We're in shock, paralysed, numb. Denial allows us to postpone the flareup of emotions. We repeat the gestures, without conviction, just trying to get to the end of the day.

Next comes anger. We feel and say terrible things, we rebel against fate, God or the people closest to us, whether they can be blamed for what happened or not. We become intractable, bitter, and aggressive; we deeply reject the situation; we want to hurt those responsible, to make them pay for what they've done. Occasionally, we intensely envy others for not having to deal with the same thing we do.

When denial is no longer possible and we get tired of the anger, negotiation comes in. We give in on some things but want to keep others. We look for some kind of agreement so that things can go back to the way they were before. We desperately try to negotiate with emotions or with those we blame for our loss, we ask for another chance. We make promises, sign pacts, negotiate deadlines.

In these three phases, the ego is tense, noticeably denser than in normal times. Even people who aren't very self-centred can become selfish at these times. The ego feels itself losing ground and desperately struggles to regain the upper hand. If it succeeds, it will gradually come out of the state of panic, and everything will return to normal. But if it doesn't, it will alternate between these various phases until it gets worn-out. This can take a long time. In these three phases, all kinds of arguments typically clash inside us. It's almost impossible to stop our minds and our thoughts run over each other. It's normal to be more distracted than usual, completely immersed in endless mental speculation.

When it becomes impossible to deny the situation, when we tire of anger and reach the limit of negotiation, there is a deep discouragement accompanied by a feeling of great loss. We feel the empty space left by the person, situation or thing we have lost, we feel it as a mutilation. We realise that our situation will never be the same again and that this change will destroy all the projects and dreams related to it. Memories of previous moments take on new worth and we may regret not having valued them enough. It then seems that we have reached the bottom, that there is only darkness ahead and that we can never be happy or at peace again. The ego finally must admit that it has lost and that all its attempts to recover have failed.

At this stage we all feel great sadness. But in some cases, rising from the ashes, the ego manages to make an unexpected turnaround. Taking hold of the despondency, it turns it into a new garment, assumes a new identity and reinforces itself in a new role. It becomes the "wretch who lost his wife", the "unfortunate who lost his job", the "victim of betrayal or injustice" and manages to come out stronger. This is how difficulties make us bitter and selfish people, disillusioned and vindictive. These sentences might sound cruel but we are not talking about you but about your ego.

It may not be easy to see the difference, because the ego's great strength lies precisely in its ability to deceive us into believing that without it we are nothing, that without it we are unprotected. But the reality is that the ego doesn't serves our interests, we serve his. And who is the ego anyway? A mirage or, as Einstein said, an optical illusion of consciousness.

In a healthy process however, the next stage is acceptance. It's the recognition of the new reality as an undeniable fact and the willingness to face the situation with an awareness of our possibilities and limitations. It's a common mistake to confuse acceptance with giving up, a state of discouragement and apparent inertia that hides a volcano of resentment. Resignation is the ego's resentful reaction to a stronger enemy, to the impossibility of recovering the part of itself that has been taken from it.

That's why I often define acceptance as surrender. The connotation this word has, at least for me, expresses very well the inner capitulation necessary for acceptance. In the four previous phases, the ego is at war; with surrender it finally signs the peace treaty, accepts and recognises its loss. Obviously, this means that it loses density and that's why, after a loss—especially if it's a big one—we can become better people, more sensitive and empathetic, more open to others.

The process of most of our losses resembles a detox process. In fact, when we look at how the ego structures itself around certain elements of its experience, we discover that, in order to survive, it creates all kinds of dependencies. I'm not just talking about drugs, alcohol or coffee; social status, comfort and even relationships are addictive and giving them up requires a period of detox. It may sound strange to say that we are addicted to someone, for example, but it happens. In break-ups, apart from the sadness of no longer seeing the person and sharing with them what we love, there is a very painful feeling–perhaps the most painful–which is that of a drug addict in a high state of abstinence. And like drug addicts, when we're in that state, we'll do anything to get our fix. That's how we often try, despite everything, to reconcile once or several times and why certain relationships, notwithstanding being deeply uncomfortable, never seem to end.

Filling the void

After acceptance there is often a kind of rebirth. We lost something, but we now feel lighter and bolder. Owning something, from the ego's point of view, always generates fear. Fear that someone else has something better, fear of spoiling it, fear of losing it. So when we lose something, we also get rid of all the fear related to what we've lost and we often feel bolder and more inclined to take risks. The period following acceptance is very productive. Whatever we've lost has left empty space and freed up time. We look for a way to fill them and are willing to try new activities or learn about issues that never aroused our interest before. It also happens that we finally find time for occupations or interests that we were never able to pursue. People at this stage are often enrolling in seminars, retreats and courses.

The seriousness of a loss is measured by the size of the void it leaves behind. It may be something apparently small, but if it is of great importance to the ego's sense of identity, it will leave a huge crater. Conversely, it may be something that people generally value, but if it's not an identity issue for the ego, the gap will quickly be filled. In cases of break-up or separation, there can be a tendency to fill the void with another relationship hastily, just because we can't bear being alone. But if we haven't mourned the previous relationship, we'll only be creating more problems for ourselves and others.

The feeling of emptiness is a threat to the ego and reminds it of how illusory and precarious its existence is and that is why it quickly tries to fill the space with anything at hand. If what we've lost has left us disappointed, if we realise that we have misplaced our trust, it's a good time to question its value. We tend to think that something has gone wrong, that someone has made a mistake, but Buddhism teaches us that because everything is impermanent, the ego's expectations of solidity, permanence and eternal happiness can never be fulfilled. So, before the ego gets tangled up in anything again, we can look for something worthwhile.

From a spiritual point of view, disenchantment with external things is excellent and, in this sense, suffering and loss are our great spiritual friends. Instead of becoming bitter towards people for not keeping their promises and being selfish, or towards things for always changing, we should realise that this is their nature, that we can't have unrealistic expectations and that, ultimately, there is no one to blame.

We can fill the spaces left by losses with more meaningful things like the development of positive qualities and emotions, dedicating at least part of the time that has become available to a spiritual practice. In this way we loosen our ego and take advantage of the opportunity life has given us to mature and grow spiritually.

When the breakdown is radical and involves losing something or someone that was very precious to us, we have the opportunity for a real fresh start. Although painful, the process is one of profound renewal and can allow us to embark on paths that, in a normal situation, we would never have chosen. Because we have freed ourselves from fear, we feel we have nothing to lose, and we must take advantage of that audacity before the ego settles back into routine. The moment of disruption is the end of something, but an opportunity to start something better.

The greatest loss

Throughout our lives we go through various phases, losing people and things and being reborn from the ashes. Some of us have experienced losses that felt like an ending, but we rarely face anything that can be compared to the prospect of our own death. Until we are confronted with it, we can't imagine the depth and radical nature of the experience. But death can be the most profound spiritual experience, the dissolution of the ego and the recognition of our true nature. There are typically three phases in approaching this prospect: chaos, surrender and transcendence.

The stages described by Elisabeth Kübler-Ross–denial, anger, negotiation, depression and acceptance–are experiences of chaos. Although these stages can be observed in all serious losses, in the context of imminent death they are felt with great intensity and follow one another in no order, back and forth, in an alternation of contradictory feelings. There are several levels of acceptance. Sometimes the first signs of acceptance are closer to resignation: recognising that there is no possibility of reversing the situation, we accept it. We still disagree but have no way of changing it. It's an antagonistic and reversible acceptance: we can still revert to anger, depression or negotiation. But it is possible to go further and give up all resistance. That's when a real transmutation takes place, and the loss becomes an initiatory and magical process of dissolving the ego. Generally, the kind of surrender necessary for this transfiguration only occurs in major losses, accidents that radically change our lives, the loss of very close loved ones or, obviously, the prospect of our own death.

Tired of resisting—and it usually takes a lot of suffering to reach this fatigue—we give up all disagreement, all struggle. We let go, we relax and surrender. After days, weeks or months of war, we choose peace: we open up instead of being defiant, we welcome instead of rejecting. We accept losing everything and... surprisingly, we discover what we've been looking for all along—even if we didn't know it. The space that opens to us is indescribable. After the storm of thoughts and the rollercoaster of emotions, we now feel a tremendous peace. A deep sense of fulfilment takes hold of us, and we feel that the boundaries of our individuality have dissolved. Surrender opens the way to transcendence: any discomfort, physical or mental, disappears and even if our body is degraded, it's just a detail. We feel such gratitude that we are immersed in unconditional love. When we reach this point, any shred of anguish or uncertainty disappears without a trace. There is total confidence that all is well. People who minister to terminally ill patients often witness this state of grace. Unfortunately, not all patients reach it.

Such abandonment can also be achieved other than at the moment of death or any other great loss. It can be due to accidental circumstances, near-death experiences or as a result of deep spiritual practice. In one way or another, and even if there is a return to a more habitual state of consciousness, this experience of selflessness inevitably produces a radical change and a weakening of the ego. The transformative power of this experience is such that even those who only witness it are touched by it. Accompanying a terminally ill patient to this stage transforms us completely.

In our habitual state, it's not easy to understand what the ego is or how it tyrannises us. We're so used to living like this that we can't understand how limited we are. If even witnessing this kind of experience in another person can transform us deeply, imagine what happens when we go to such an experience ourselves!

As soon as this fictitious structure we call the ego dissolves, it's as if the water of a container is released and returns to the ocean. The feeling of separation that we've harboured all our life (which we've unconsciously cultivated through all the ego's strategies) dissolves and our spacious consciousness expands without limits. It's very simple, but it takes a lot of suffering to get there. See how vigorously most of us resist having the slightest thing taken away from us, how angrily we react to the slightest threat. The ego resists as long as it can, and its energy is immense. We can beat it through erosion, but it takes time. That's why great losses are true blessings.

Growing old

If death and the great losses of our lives are sudden opportunities for the dissolution of identity, ageing is a progressive dissolution. This process, which began much earlier a few centuries ago, has now been slowed down by a few years. Thanks to healthcare, comfort, hygiene and lifestyle, we have more years to live and can remain active for longer. We aren't toothless, wrinkled and bowed like our ancestors; we can easily hide our grey hair and have many ways to fool ourselves about our age. But sooner or later we must admit the successive losses of identity. It can be difficult to accept that our memory fails us, that we can no longer do what we used to do. Even if we were an expert in our field, knowledge evolves, technology develops and soon we are outdated and relegated. Others take our place, run our businesses and do it their way. In our society where people are defined by what they do, to stop being productive is annihilation.

Even if we are lucky enough to have children or loving family members, we must be prepared for the difficulty of becoming dependent. During our adult life, we might have felt we didn't need anyone and that we could make our own decisions, but we will reach a point where everyone seems to know better than us what we can and can't do. In addition to disabilities and physical pain, we can see the decline of our intellectual capacities. Our personal world shrinks day by day and people no longer seek our company. If we attach too much importance to our physical appearance, we live in perpetual frustration at seeing that beauty has gone and we are most reluctant to look at ourselves in the mirror. When our physical dependence becomes great, and we need others to feed us, change our nappy or help us bathe, there is little left of our usual arrogance. No wonder many of us feel this as an assault on our dignity and take revenge for these humiliations by becoming petty, suspicious and controlling.

If, from the ego's point of view, growing old is terrifying, from a spiritual point of view it can be a great opportunity. As more and more elements of our identity fall away, the ego breaks down and grows weaker. Titles, opinions, social status or beauty, which used to inspire us with pride and which we were so afraid of losing, show how little they are worth. We see how the struggles we were involved in for a social position or career advancement have turned out to be in vain and we regret having wasted so much time and energy on them. Towards the end of her life, I remember my mum saying, "I don't know why people spend so much energy arguing. We're here for such a short time that it's a waste". As the ego no longer has anything to hold onto–if we accept it with openness and a sense of humour–the natural luminosity of our mind begins to radiate.

Although it's rare in today's society, I have seen this extraordinary abandonment in the eyes of some elderly people. With the abandonment of the ego comes a great tenderness and we feel as if everyone is our child or grandchild. All the suffering we see around us seems such a waste and it becomes hard to understand how we can argue for things that aren't really worth it. When we feel that tenderness, we will not see becoming dependent on others as something that deprives us of our dignity. As babies we only survived thanks to others. If we hadn't had someone to feed, protect and care for us, we would have died in just a few hours. When we reach adulthood, we think that we no longer need others, but at the end of our lives we return to our original condition. Actually, we were never independent–we just thought we were. We think that generosity only consists of giving, but we must be generous in order to receive. It's only when we see how difficult it can be that we realise that there was a hidden arrogance in giving. Receiving is more difficult because it seems to place us in a position of inferiority.

The bigger and denser our ego is, the more fear it has of disappearing. In these conditions, growing old is a terror and that's why many of us are ready to do anything to maintain the illusion that we're still young and still in shape. We resist as hard as we can the successive losses caused by age and try to compensate for those we can't avoid with grumpiness. In the natural order of things, this weakening of the ego brings wisdom—not just the knowledge that results from life experience, but above all the radiance of the natural goodness of our mind.

This process will be much easier if, during our existence, we have developed a deeper recognition of our true nature. If we have lived with kindness, practiced meditation and understood the reality of the world, the peeling away of the ego will be natural and progressive. We won't attach so much importance to all the things it identifies with, and therefore it won't be such a big drama to lose those things. From a spiritual point of view, growing old is another of our great blessings.

Empathy and compassion

Sometimes we wonder if Buddhism is right when it says that human beings are naturally good. It doesn't take much: you only have to switch on the television news to have serious doubts! But if we've been lucky enough to go through an experience in which the ego has lost density, we stop doubting. Fear, depression, attachment and all the emotions that usually tear us apart disappear as if by magic, leaving us face to face with the indescribable beauty of our nature. To a greater or lesser degree, any experience in which the ego loses its grip brings us closer to our fundamental nature, and empathy, tenderness and compassion manifest effortlessly. That's why even those with no spiritual training can naturally make sense of and transform their suffering by opening up to others and feeling empathy.

It's common for people in desperate situations to cope by finding a purpose that goes beyond them. Thus, in natural disasters, accidents or wars, strangers who would normally feel suspicious help each other–barriers fall and with them the concepts that feed the feeling of separation. The other is recognised as an equal and empathy arises effortlessly. When we think we've reached the limit of our strength, it can seem strange to help others. From the ego's point of view, if we don't have the energy to help ourselves, how can we help someone else? However, if the ego barrier falls, we have access to a wealth of energy that we never imagined we had. It's not uncommon for this to happen and for people to break out of the impasse in which they are by focusing on others. The following story is one of my favourites.

During a war, a group of refugees set off from a village towards the border. As they were made up of energetic young people, they kept up a good pace and had a good chance of crossing the border before being caught by the invading army. As they passed through a village however, a girl with a baby and an old man begged to join them. Of course, accepting them into the group carried risks and reduced their chances of reaching the border safe and sound. On the other hand, to leave them behind was to condemn them.

After discussing it among themselves, the group decided to take the risk. However, they set two conditions: each person would take the baby in turn and if the elderly man couldn't keep up, he would be left behind. The newcomers accepted the conditions and joined the group. The days passed and, although the elderly man had some difficulty keeping up, everything went well. After a few days, however, he became utterly exhausted and said he couldn't keep up. "Please, as agreed, carry on without me. I'll be fine."

They were dismayed. Now that they had bonded, nobody wanted to leave him, but it wasn't possible to take him either. They stood there not knowing what to do until the young woman put the baby in his arms, saying "You can't give up, today it's your turn to take him!" With tears in his eyes, the old man picked up the child, stood up and started walking.

When we think we've reached the limit of our strength and can't take another step, surprisingly, altruistic motivation makes us go beyond the limitations imposed by the ego. What we don't do for ourselves, we do for others with joy. This is the paradox of human nature. In normal conditions, under the dominion of the ego, we can be petty and selfish, but when faced with truly difficult situations, the best of ourselves can appear.

When we're in a difficult situation, we should remember that if we give in to depression and anger, we're not plunging alone. We're taking family and friends with us, the people we love most and who care about us. If you're suffering because you feel you've become a burden to them, try to make it easier for them by gaining the courage to respond better. Remember that there are hundreds and thousands of people suffering right now, some in far worse situations than yours. Even if you can't do anything for them, you can wish you could and vow that their suffering ends right now. At the very least, your example of courage in the face of adversity can be an inspiration to others.

Empathy and solidarity ease the torment of the ego. We constantly see people who have experienced great loss overcome their difficulties by putting themselves at the service of others. Depending on their means and abilities, they can, for example, become volunteers, share their experiences in support groups or create solidarity structures such as foundations or charities. Whatever the external dimension of help, empathy and solidarity bring us closer to our kind nature and counteract the illusion of the ego.

Ringu Tulku Rinpoche often tells the story of a lady who, after a car accident, became a paraplegic. Since she couldn't accept the situation, she felt so angry that her life and that of her family and friends became a living hell. Tortured and depressed, she began to think about suicide. One day, in town, she saw a legless beggar on a wooden plank with four wheels. Despite his disability and poverty, the man seemed to be smiling a lot, addressing people in a friendly and joyous way. Many seemed to know him and responded with affection. "It's incredible," she thought, "this man is in a much worse situation than me and yet he seems happy!"

She returned home and she kept thinking of the beggar. She felt so ashamed of her own attitude that she promised herself not to let a single day go by without doing something for someone. From that day on, when she woke up in the morning, instead of thinking about her unhappiness, she thought: "What can I do today to help someone?" At first it was difficult to find something to do every day, but over time she began to do not just one thing, but two, three, ten. After a few weeks, she completely lost the desire to kill herself and discovered that life really was worth living. As time went by, she stopped feeling angry about what had happened to her and began thinking what a blessing it had been, she was now a much better person and her life had greater meaning.

You may think it's impossible to feel gratitude for bad things, but the truth is that when they weaken the grip of our ego, they make us better and happier people. That's why it's common for people to recognise the spiritual value of difficulties.

Contemplation and Prayer

Whenever the ego loses ground, it's a good time to turn inwards. All the world's religions talk about prayer, each in its own way. Even if we don't belong to any religion or don't understand prayer, it is possible to turn inwards and access the stillness within. Through meditation we can train in awareness but then go deeper to discover unknown dimensions of ourselves. What we generally know of the mind is merely the whirlwind of perceptions, thoughts and emotions but, when we deeply relax, we can touch the depths of an extraordinary stillness.

When we are distressed, anxious or tense, we feel a constriction, a lump in the throat or chest and a sensation of breathlessness. The origin of the word anguish is the Latin *angere,* which means to tighten, to constrict. This constriction, both physical and mental, narrows our perspective on things, so that the slightest problem is seen as a catastrophe. As soon as our mind relaxes and opens to the present moment, we experience a feeling of inner openness and expansion. Thoughts don't vanish, but as our consciousness becomes much more spacious, the feeling of constriction disappears. Suddenly, there is space around the thoughts and, naturally, they lose much of their importance. While we're in this tight spot, we identify with our thoughts, thinking that they are who we are. When we discover this inner space, we realise that we are much more than that. Consciousness is a spacious and vast sky, our thoughts are just passing clouds.

Shifting from the clouds to the sky generates a feeling of stability and security that is the opposite of the agitation and insecurity produced by the frenzy of mental states. Whether they are good or bad, pleasant or unpleasant, it doesn't change the sky at all. Another example is that of a crystal. The crystal is transparent but can appear blue if placed on a blue surface. In the same way, our consciousness can take on all kinds of colours, shapes and patterns, depending on the thoughts on which it rests. Its essence, however, remains unchanged.

Visualising images can be a powerful way of working on and transforming our perspective of a problem. To do this, we can use an idea, image or mental representation which, through the feelings it inspires, brings about a profound transformation in our state of mind. Thus, a religious person can evoke a spiritual being, a deity or a concept related to their own belief. A non-religious person could choose any form or any element such as the sun, the moon, the ocean, fire, etc., as long as they recognise it as a positive force or essence. It must be something that makes sense and naturally produces a feeling of calm and trust. If we had the opportunity to familiarise ourselves with its meaning and appearance, it will be all the easier to use it as a source of power.

In Tibetan Buddhism, the sources of power can be the expression of certain qualities of our mind, such as compassion, wisdom or the power of transformation, in the form of a deity, a syllable or a *mantra*. It can also be a prayer or the formulation of a life ideal, such as this stanza from Langri Thangpa[11] : "If someone treats me badly out of envy, slanders me, offends me or causes me other harm, I will learn to take defeat upon myself and offer them victory."

At the end of the book you'll find a visualisation you can use, the Meditation on the Source of Power. Adapt it to you, make it your own using the symbols or the meaning that suits your feelings.

Intention and positive emotions

Since suffering triggers very strong negative emotions, it must be countered with equally intense positive emotions in order to be transformed. The classical texts call the thought that triggers these positive emotions an antidote.

It's not uncommon for people who are suffering to spontaneously think: "I don't wish this harm on anyone." This is a compassionate thought and if it makes sense to you, cultivate it until you no longer feel any disagreement or resistance. When you feel comfortable with it, go further. Think something like: "Since I'm already suffering, how nice it would be if no-one else had to go through the same thing! May all similar problems be absorbed on mine and may all those who are suffering be released immediately!" If you feel resistance to thinking something like this, realise that it's

---

[11] Tibetan master famous for having written a short poem known as "The Eight Stanzas of Langri Thangpa".

not about increasing your suffering, but about making it useful and meaningful. Wouldn't it be nice to be able to exhaust the suffering of others without any inconvenience to yourself? Let this feeling become real and sincere, until you feel a deep joy that brings tears to your eyes. Then you'll realise that your suffering seems much lighter and almost non-existent.

You can also practise an exercise Tibetans call *tonglen*—give and take. This practice consists of using the back and forth of the breath to inhale the suffering of others and exchange it for our own happiness. It is so simple that it could even be described as simplistic. However, its transformative power is fabulous.

In the 1980s Khyentse Rinpoche, one of the greatest masters of Tibetan Buddhism, had the opportunity to return to Tibet for the first time after his exile in India. During this trip, he met with old friends who had stayed in Tibet and with whom he had not been in contact. One of them, a prisoner of the Chinese for several years, told him that he had only managed to survive and maintain his sanity thanks to this practice. He said that the torture sessions left him physically broken, but what tortured him most was the permanent anguish of never knowing when they would start again. Feeling that he was losing his mind, he desperately searched for a way to deal with the situation. Although he had never been much of a practitioner, he remembered hearing the explanation of this practice and decided to apply it. He began to meditate in this way, expressing his vow to take on the suffering of others and send happiness to them. Over time, he managed to free himself from all anguish, so that every time they came to pick him up, he was without apprehension, at peace, and almost joyful. It may seem impossible for a simple practice like this to have such power, but the most important factor is the degree of motivation of the practitioner. In this case, Khyentse Rinpoche's friend was so desperate that he dedicated himself to this practice with all his heart and soul.

People often ask whether it's possible to take on the suffering of others and alleviate the pain of those for whom we practise. It's not impossible. There are studies that demonstrate the power of prayers in treatment and healing. But we must realise that although we can't be sure of the effect it will have on others, we can easily see the power to transform and give meaning to our own suffering.

The main aim of this practice is to do something that is completely counter-intuitive to the ego: not only do we accept suffering—which is already a huge blow—but we exchange our happiness for the suffering of others, something totally unthinkable. In this way, by releasing the grip of the ego, our suffering is immediately transformed. You'll also find a guided meditation for practicing *tonglen* at the end of the book.

The one taste

In his day, Buddha was known for his smile, and even today his depictions show him with a serene, slightly smiling face. His expression is captivating and perhaps that's why Buddha's images have become so fashionable. But what does it really express?

As far as we can see, what makes Buddha smile is the realisation of the nature of self and of phenomena and, through this, the liberation from all misunderstandings and all conflicting emotions such as fear, desire, anger, aversion. Although it's hard to imagine what our life would be like without them, it's easy to understand how comfortable it must be. If the state of Buddhahood is characterised, among other things, by a total absence of fear and a transcendence of all suffering, what can we—who are not yet Buddhas—hope to achieve? The teachings of Tibetan Buddhism use the expression *ronyam,* the one taste.

As a result of successful spiritual practice, experienced practitioners achieve a serene tranquility in which all things are seen as they are, neither dramatic nor fantastic. The more the ego has lost ground, the less life's events are seen through its eyes and, consequently, the less they are polarised in terms of aversion and desire. There is no more need to run to or from anything. What remains is far from dull, it's the rich, colourful, throbbing texture of life itself.

Experienced practitioners approach life with an even keeled attitude in which there is only one taste. Not in the sense that everything has lost so much of its salt that it ends up tasting the same, but in the sense that they appreciate the bitter, the sweet and all the flavours of life with the same openness and kindness. Being completely one with every moment, they don't fear or desire it, but just enjoy it.

But if you don't think that's within your reach either, what could be? I have seen from experience that practising the methods detailed here leads, in time, to a form of confident serenity. In everyday life, we react well to ordinary challenges and don't lose patience so easily. In difficult moments, we find elegant exits and ways to avoid unnecessary suffering more quickly. In general, we approach life with the confidence that whatever happens, we'll be able to handle it. Or, as Ringu Tulku puts it: "Everything is ok even if it's not ok."

This doesn't mean that we no longer fear suffering or that we no longer aspire to happiness, but neither prospect distresses us too much. Realising that everything is impermanent, we know that both have a lifespan. We know that life is not black and white and that adverse circumstances can contribute as much or more than favourable ones to our well-being and happiness.

The courage to recognise the reality of suffering allows us to demystify the monster, gives us greatness and makes us compassionate and empathetic. We no longer need to mask the truths of life with trivialities, and so we gain depth and human warmth. We enjoy our own company and attract others. We create affectionate, deep bonds that are not based on a tangle of wearisome emotions but on natural heart-to-heart connectivity. And if that isn't happiness, I don't know what is!

Practical tips from chapter 7

- Suffering is a spiritual awakener.
- Loss, when accepted, makes us better people.
- Fill the void left by loss with the spiritual path.
- What we don't do for ourselves, we do for others with joy.
- Cultivate a strong positive intention.
- Exchange your happiness for the suffering of others.
- Gain the confidence that you will be able to deal with whatever happens.

· CHAPTER 8 ·

GROW YOUR OWN HAPPINESS

There is a place inside us where happiness already lives, independent from any external condition. Love, compassion and joy are the natural qualities of our mind but, because we are caught in our mental struggles, we fail to recognise them and feel miserable. This is why, growing our own happiness is more about removing what prevents it from naturally shining forward than artificially building something from scratch.

Firstly, we must become aware of all the habitual negative patterns that plague us and replace them with more positive ones. Once we gather the basic conditions of well-being, we then open our hearts and let compassion, joy, gratitude and love grow organically. The problem is that, in our view of the world, adversities and problems are the destroyers of happiness. They inherently oppose each other so that where they are present there can be no joy. However, much of the suffering we experience when confronted with adversities and problems doesn't come from them but is self-inflicted through lack of awareness and perspective. And this is why, in this book there has been so much reference to suffering that you may feel that happiness was forgotten.

We have seen people who go through terrible hardships and never despair, who are still loving, grateful and happy. It is a mistake to imagine that we can only be happy when all the problems and difficulties we face are solved—because that will never happen. Even if, for a brief moment, all seems well, something else will come up to spoil the party. We must learn how to take everything in our stride, without constantly delaying happiness.

I have lived for quite a few decades and have experienced many trials and tribulations, but I, fortunately, found Buddhism early in life and this has given me the tools to transform my suffering into happiness. For someone who, in her teens, realised she wasn't very good at being happy, this is quite an achievement. If I did it, so can you! Thanks to the Buddhist teachings I have understood that, if we constantly fear, suffering will spoil whatever enjoyment we have, we can never relax and be at peace. Our fear and rejection of suffering can be so strong that it is actually the fear and rejection themselves that make us suffer the most. And that is why we must have a good look at suffering, recognise its causes, learn to accept it and eventually transform it.

For us to develop a level of happiness that can encompass suffering, we need to let our hearts grow bigger. If we don't feel the connection with others and don't have a purpose that goes beyond our self-interest it will be very difficult to achieve this. Developing compassion and kindness and becoming involved in altruistic endeavours will naturally make our lives significant. With a sense of purpose everything in life gains meaning and we realise that it is both through happiness and suffering that we gain depth as human beings. We can then let go of fear, develop acceptance, gratitude and trust.

To walk this path from where we are today, we need to look first at our past, to forgive our own mistakes and the mistakes of others, to accept the difficulties we faced but without dwelling on them. We let go but with a determination to do better, to become a more compassionate person, to live a more altruistic life. In the present we must now accept what we cannot change and change what we can. We accept that life is not fixed but always moving and changing. We find the courage to accept all setbacks by looking at the impermanence of life and the inevitability of being hit by the bullets of trauma. Now is the time to grow our hearts, nurture ourselves with learning and make commitments to change our behaviour towards others as well as ourselves. Through Buddhist teachings and meditation we make ourselves better prepared to handle, give meaning to and transform whatever is thrown at us, with grace, compassion and love.

This is the way we grow stronger and more resilient, and ultimately, cultivate happiness today and for the future. There is much to learn but so much more to be gained. Regular meditation gives us perspective which becomes the basis to see things in a positive light, without fear or worry, knowing that we have the tools to deal with any suffering and still find ways to help others deal with their difficulties, using compassion and kindness. Taking the right steps now will open the door to a future filled with beauty, joy, peace, love and true happiness.

Remember that you being happy, in itself, makes the world a better place. By touching others in positive ways you enrich their lives, benefitting everyone. Think positive thoughts, speak positively and act in a positive way. No more feeding the ego with negativity and self-centredness, open your heart to see all the places you can find happiness:–making someone smile or feel better about themselves, giving help or accepting help, knowing that you can handle any situation, loving yourself but still being able to put others first, feeling grateful for every aspect of life, forgiving yourself as well as others, understanding who you really are and still being amazed at what you can achieve.

But don't forget all the sights, sounds, smells, tastes and feelings of the external world that lift our hearts to a place where we truly feel happy:–hearing a baby's first giggle, visiting incredible places, being cuddled by a pet, reading an inspiring book, seeing someone show their passion for life, viewing beautiful art, achieving a dream at work or in sport, finding the peace and spaciousness within yourself through meditation.

Happiness awaits, begin the cultivation process today!

• APPENDIX •

GUIDED MEDITATIONS

Scattered throughout this book there are many clues and explanations about meditation. However, it might be useful to summarise everything, giving some instructions for specific meditations in a dedicated chapter.

Generally speaking, meditation is a training to shift our attention from thinking to something that connects us to the here and now. It could be an external object such as a candle flame, a flower or a picture; it could be the perception of the sounds around us; it could be the physical sensations we are experiencing. One of the most widely used techniques is observing your own breathing.

The idea is to observe that inner or outer object. But observing doesn't mean commenting: "The candle is almost out"; "The neighbour has come home"; "My leg is numb". Observing is paying attention, becoming fully aware: feeling the breath, hearing the sounds, seeing the form. Of course, thoughts are constantly interrupting and, because of habit, we go after them. Whenever we realise this, we go back to the object of our observation. Meditation is not a fight against thoughts; bringing our attention back is not an arm wrestle. Imagine that you suddenly realise you're walking around the house carrying a heavy bag. You don't have to fight it, just put it down. When you bring your attention back, you do something similar, you let go of your thoughts and relax.

If you feel a lot of tension, it's probably because you're fighting your thoughts and feeling irritated at not being able to stay alert. Relax, take a short break. Taking a break isn't about getting up making a cup of tea or checking if an email has arrived. Taking a break is just relaxing, letting your mind run, stretching your legs or making a few slow movements. At first, the stability of awareness is very fragile, so the slightest physical movement can generate mental turbulence. Be careful not to take too long breaks that give the mind the freedom to get involved in a chain of thoughts. A few seconds is more than enough.

Many people think that meditation consists of emptying the mind of thoughts, make it blank. Although it's natural for our mind to calm down after some practice, there will always be thoughts. Just as there is always movement on the surface of even the calmest water, there is always movement in the mind. Meditation doesn't serve to put an end to thoughts, but to discover that we have freedom and don't need to be manipulated by them. We don't follow them, we don't fight them—we are just aware of them.

This aware and spacious presence is a key point of meditation. People often think that meditation is a way of detaching from reality. That's what we do all the time when we get caught up in endless chains of thoughts! In mindfulness we do the opposite: we look at reality, we open ourselves up to what is happening right here, right now.

The other key point of meditation is relaxation. If we approach meditation in a very tense way, meditating will be a torment. We must learn to make meditation a pleasant moment during which we unwind and relax. Sometimes, if we are tired or tense, relaxation can lead us to a state of pleasant numbness in which there are no thoughts, and we feel good. This state is not synonymous with meditation, it is more like the prelude to falling asleep. Although it is relaxing and pleasant, it has an element of mental torpor that is very different from the sharp, awake presence of meditation. If we feel ourselves sinking into this state, we should open our eyes (if we're meditating with our eyes closed) or lift our gaze (if we're meditating with your eyes open directed downwards). We could take a few deep breaths or do a series of breathing exercises like the ones I'll explain later. Or just let ourselves go and take a nap, if that is what we need!

Many people become discouraged when they realise that, even after a while, they still have meditation sessions in which they are completely distracted, in great inner turmoil. I have seen that the results of meditation manifest themselves more quickly in everyday life than during the sessions. So don't judge your progress that way. Persevere. Start with a few minutes of meditation. Ten minutes a day is enough to make a difference and is preferable to half an hour just one day a week. As with any other discipline, regularity is paramount. When you feel more comfortable, gradually increase the time.

The mind works with habits and rituals. For example, every day when we get up, we go to the bathroom, wash our face, brush our teeth, have breakfast, etc. We should do the same with meditation. Choose a room or a corner of the house where you feel good and it's more peaceful. Create a little ritual: light a candle and a stick of incense, close the curtains (a little darkness helps internalisation), sit in a certain posture. All these gestures become a routine that gradually helps you overcome the ups and downs, the fluctuations and the occasional slump.

Meditation is an exercise that everyone must do for themselves. Meditation courses and classes set you in the right direction, give you the confidence that you're not making mistakes and allow you to dispel any doubts. If you can, go to a credible school and seek guidance from an instructor. Experience has shown me that many people enjoy meditating in a group and attend classes, but don't practise on their own. One meditation session a week is far from enough. So, whether you can follow group meditations or not, try to meditate at home for at least ten minutes a day.

I realise that, for various reasons, not everyone is able to follow group classes or meditations. That's why I've included here some basic instructions to get you started on your own. The first levels of meditation are actually quite simple and there isn't much danger you can go wrong.

The following guided meditations can guide you through the first steps. Follow the instructions or record them in your own voice and transfer them to an mp3 player or your phone.

You can also download some of the recorded meditations on my website www.tseringpaldron.com/eng

Use the recordings for as long as you feel you need. Recordings are useful in that they create a temporal structure and also bring you back through the sound of the voice, never letting your thoughts stray too far. On the other hand, after a few times, they can become monotonous and repetitive. The ideal, in any case, is to meditate by yourself.

Posture

Sit cross-legged on a mat or sofa. Use a cushion under your hips to elevate them, if that's more comfortable. Sit on the edge of the cushion or use a wedge cushion so that your pelvis tilts forwards, creating a curve in your kidneys. In this way, your back straightens effortlessly. If you are using a Zafu (Japanese round cushion) you can use it vertically, like riding it. You can also use a meditation bench.

If this posture is too uncomfortable, sit on a chair, sofa or lean back in bed. If your physical condition doesn't allow for any other position, lie down.

If you're sitting, try to straighten your back.

Keep your shoulders slightly pulled down and back.

Place the cervical vertebrae and the head on the extension of the spine.

Tuck your chin in slightly.

Place your hands on your knees, palms down, or place them on your lap, right hand on top of your left, palms facing up, the tips of your thumbs together.

Stick the tongue to the palate, the tip touching the upper teeth on the inside.

You can leave your eyes open or close them, depending on how you feel best.

Try to relax your body, avoiding unnecessary tension, and relax your mind, letting go of thoughts about the past or the future.

Give up speculation and focus only on the here and now.

Connect with the present moment by feeling the sounds, smells and various sensations that are happening.

Decide that all problems and all projects can wait.

Formulate your intention for the next few minutes.

TSERING PALDRON

Breathing exercise

If you like, you can do some breathing exercises that will help stabilise your mind. There are many ways to do them. The following description is just one of them.

- Press the base of the ring finger of each hand with the tip of your thumb. This gesture helps transform negative energy into positive energy, pessimism into optimism.
- Close the other fingers and place your hands back on your knees, with the backs of your hands facing upwards.
- Inhale deeply, raise your right hand to face level and, keeping your thumb in place, block your left nostril with your ring finger and exhale through your right nostril.
- In synchronisation with the exhalation, gradually open your left hand, which is resting on your knee.
- At the end of the exhalation, force out the rest of the air still in your lungs by contracting your diaphragm and fully extending the fingers of your left hand, as if you were stretching.
- As you exhale, consider releasing the tensions caused by aversion. Visualise them as dirty white smoke coming out of your right nostril.
- Close your hands again and rest them on your knees.
- Inhale. Raise your left hand and block your right nostril with your left ring finger.
- Exhale as before, thinking that you are releasing all the tensions linked to attachment, visualising them as dark red smoke coming

out of your left nostril. Open the fingers of your right hand progressively as you exhale.
- Clasp your hands as before and rest them on your knees.
- Inhale for the third time. Exhale through both nostrils, opening your hands, which are resting on your knees. Think that you are releasing the tensions created by pessimism, sadness and insecurity and visualise them as a blue-grey smoke coming out of your nostrils.

This cycle of three breaths can be done once, three times, nine times or more. If you feel particularly agitated or confused, you can repeat it more times, but without forcing it. At the end, check your posture, correct it if necessary, and relax any tensions that may have arisen. Bring your awareness to the present moment.

Refuge and Four Boundless Thoughts

In the supreme Buddha, Dharma and assembly
I take Refuge until attaining enlightenment.
Through the merit of practicing Generosity and so on,
May I attain Buddhahood in order to benefit beings.

May all beings have happiness and the causes of happiness;
May they all be free from suffering and the causes of suffering;
May they never be deprived of happiness devoid of any suffering;
May they abide in great impartiality, free from attachment to others.

Guided meditations

The purpose of Shamatha, or Calm Abiding Meditation, is to stabilise the mind by cultivating a steady awareness of the object of meditation. The traditional practice of Shamatha uses different kinds of supports or anchors for our practice, but breathing meditation is by far the most widely used technique. Here are 3 alternatives for concentrating on your breathing. Try them all and alternate or choose the one that feels most comfortable.

Breathing meditation A

- Focus your attention on the coming and going of your breath. Don't get lost in conjecture: Am I supposed to breathe like this? or faster? or deeper? Breathe normally, without forcing, and be aware.

- Count your breaths. Whenever you realise you're following your thoughts, bring your attention back and start counting again. Try to get to 10. If you succeed (unlikely at first), start counting again.
- When you bring your attention back, do it in a relaxed way. Don't fight the thoughts. Don't follow them. Just let them go.
- At the end, inhale deeply and, as you exhale, come back. Stretch your legs and arms. Stand up slowly with no rush.

Breathing meditation B

- Focus on the coming and going of your breath. Breathe normally, without forcing it.
- Notice a sensation connected to breathing. Perhaps the sensation of air passing through your nostrils, the movement of your chest, the filling and emptying of your lungs. Choose the sensation that makes the most sense to you.
- When you bring your attention back to this sensation, do it in a relaxed way. Don't fight the thoughts. Don't follow them. Abandon them as soon as you realise they are there, like someone putting down an object they have inadvertently picked up.
- At the end, inhale deeply and, as you exhale, come back. Stretch your legs and arms. Stand up slowly.

Breathing meditation C

- Focus on the coming and going of your breath. Breathe normally, without forcing it.

- Feel the rhythm of this movement, a coming and going, similar to that of the waves. Feel yourself being rocked by it and let go.
- Observe how the air flows in and out.
- Centre yourself in the chest area and imagine that you are breathing with your heart. Imagine it expanding when you breathe in and contracting when you breathe out.
- Every time you breathe out, feel yourself emptying your body of all tension.
- When you bring your attention back, do it in a relaxed way. Don't fight the thoughts; don't follow them; let them go.
- At the end, inhale deeply and, as you exhale, come back. Stretch your legs and arms. Stand up slowly.

Meditation on sensations

- Focus on the coming and going of your breath for a few seconds. Breathe normally, without forcing it. With each exhalation, empty yourself of all tension.
- Feel your body as a set of present sensations and not as a mental representation. Become aware of your posture and the sensations related to it.
- Feel your feet–don't imagine them, feel them. Contract them. Relax and feel them again.
- Feel your legs. Contract them. Relax and feel them again.
- Feel your buttocks. Contract them. Relax and feel them again.
- Feel your abdomen. Contract it. Relax and feel it again.
- Feel your chest. Contract it. Relax and feel it again.
- Feel your back. Contract it. Relax and feel it again.

- Feel your shoulders. Contract them. Relax and feel them again.
- Feel your arms. Contract them. Relax and feel them again.
- Feel your hands. Contract them. Relax and feel them again.
- Feel your neck. Contract it. Relax and feel it again.
- Feel your scalp. Contract it. Relax and feel it again.
- Feel your forehead. Contract it. Relax and feel it again.
- Feel your eyelids. Contract them. Relax and feel them again.
- Feel your cheekbones. Contract them. Relax and feel them again.
- Feel your lips. Contract them. Relax and feel them again.
- Feel your chin. Contract it. Relax and feel it again.
- Feel how the energy flows through your body and feel how alive it is. You may feel a slight tingling sensation.
- Observe any sensations that occur and feel them as they are without focus too much on identifying them. Don't just think: "I feel itchy". Take a moment to look at the sensation. What is it really? Feel it without judgement.
- At the end, inhale deeply and, as you exhale, come back. Stretch your legs and arms. Stand up slowly.

Meditation on sounds

- Focus on the coming and going of your breath for a few seconds. Breathe normally, without forcing it. With each exhalation, empty yourself of all tension.
- Pay attention to the sounds around you. Whether it's honking horns or birds chirping, observe them without evaluation or judgement.

- Just hear to what there is to listen to as *sound*. Whether you like or dislike it, focus on the sound quality of what you're hearing. Imagine you are a newborn baby and you've never heard these sounds before.
- Choose a sound, constant or intermittent, and concentrate on it for a moment. If you feel any irritation, relax.
- Choose a distant or faint sound and concentrate on it for a moment.
- At the end, inhale deeply and, as you exhale, come back. Stretch your legs and arms. Stand up slowly.

Meditation on space

- Focus on the coming and going of breath for a few seconds. Breathe normally, without forcing it. With each exhalation, empty yourself of all tension.
- Choose the technique that works best for you: breathing, sensations or sounds until you stabilise your awareness.
- When you bring your attention back, do it in a relaxed way. Don't fight the thoughts; don't follow them; let them go.
- When you start to feel an inner opening, like a spacious, clear and present awareness, focus your attention on it.
- Feel that the alternation between spacious awareness and thought mode is a natural movement, don't get irritated by it.
- Relax whenever you return to spacious awareness and feel that thoughts are just passing events, like clouds in the sky.
- At the end, inhale deeply and, as you exhale, come back. Stretch your legs and arms. Stand up slowly.

Instant meditation – three conscious breaths

Wherever you are, whatever position you're in, while you're waiting for the traffic light to turn green, the computer to start up, or any other situation, you can pause for three breaths. Take these breaks as often as you remember. To help you remember, set a reminder on your mobile phone.

- Wherever you are, in whatever position, tune into the state of awareness.
- You don't need to close your eyes or get into any special position. Just straighten your back slightly and feel the space around you. Become aware of some distant sounds and feel your breath. Take three conscious breaths.
- Resume your activity.

TSERING PALDRON

Meditation to set an intention at the beginning of the day

Choose the moment that seems most favourable before you start your day. It could be as soon as you wake up, after you've washed your face and cleaned your teeth, before you've had breakfast or afterwards. You can combine this practice with Shamatha meditation. For example, do 10 or 15 minutes of Shamatha and conclude with this practice.

- Sit in meditation posture, on the floor, on the bed or on a chair
- Do some breathing exercises
- Focus on your breathing, using whichever technique you prefer.
- Remember the purpose of your life: to try to become more present, more aware, a better person for yourself and for others.
- Consider the day's activities beforehand as opportunities to implement new attitudes or correct old habits. Open yourself up to the events of the day, whether they are pleasant or unpleasant.
- Use a personal formula, for example: "May I reconcile the good of others with my own today. May I not harm anyone and, on the contrary, may I help in any way I can". Use your own words, from the bottom of your heart.
- At the end, relax for a few seconds without concentrating on anything specifically. Then inhale deeply and come back as you exhale. Stretch your legs and arms. Stand up slowly.

Meditation to review your day

At the end of the day, whether before going to bed or already lying down, review your day. You can combine this practice with meditation. For example, do 10 or 15 minutes of meditation and conclude with this practice.

- Sit in meditation posture, on the floor, on the bed or on a chair.
- Do some breathing exercises.
- Focus on your breathing, using whichever technique you prefer.
- Remember the purpose of your life: to try to become more present, more aware, a better person.
- Review your day without judgement or blame. See how well you reacted at certain moments and congratulate yourself. Decide that you want to continue on this path and do better tomorrow.
- Look at how you haven't reacted well at other times. Think about how you could have reacted better. Decide that you want to keep trying to improve your reactions.
- Finish your day and dedicate your efforts to achieving your goal: becoming a more aware, kinder and happier person.

Meditation on impermanence

- Sit in meditation posture, on the floor, on the bed or on a chair.
- Do some breathing exercises.
- Focus on your breathing, sensations or sounds. Use whichever technique you prefer.

- When you've achieved some peace of mind, think about a change that has taken place recently. Don't speculate and don't let your thoughts carry you away. Let yourself be immersed in the realisation of the change.
- Consider what is happening in your life today and ask yourself if you could have imagined it a few years ago. Let yourself be immersed in the realisation of change.
- Look for an example of impermanence that has marked you and let it permeate you.
- At the end, relax for a few seconds without concentrating on anything specific. Then inhale deeply and come back as you exhale. Stretch your legs and arms. Stand up slowly.

Meditation on gratitude

- Sit in meditation posture, on the floor, on the bed or on a chair.
- Do some breathing exercises.
- Focus on your breathing, sensations or sounds. Use whichever technique you prefer.
- When you've achieved some calmness, think about something for which you are grateful. Don't speculate and don't let your thoughts carry you away. Let gratitude permeate you.
- If the feeling starts to fade or you're carried away by thoughts, bring your attention back and remember something else for which you feel grateful. Let the feeling sink in.
- Continue the exercise, reminding yourself of all the good things in your life and feeling more and more grateful.

- At the end, relax for a few seconds without concentrating on anything specific. Then inhale deeply and come back as you exhale. Stretch your legs and arms. Stand up slowly.

Pain-orientated mindfulness meditation

- Start by putting your body in as comfortable a position as possible, sitting on a chair, lying on the bed or on the floor. Relax, feel the weight of your body come down, as if you were going to melt into the earth, and take a few deep breaths, exhaling all tension.
- Allow the breath to get into its natural rhythm. Observe how the chest opens and closes, the abdomen rises and falls. If your breathing has been affected by illness or pain, observe it with kindness. Let go of ideas about how things should be and accept them as they are, here and now.
- Feel your breathing like the coming and going of a wave: you don't have to interfere or be afraid, just let it happen. Associate the exhale with the moment when the wave spreads out and feel yourself relax more with each exhale. If you have another image that makes sense and helps you relax, use it.
- Notice how each breath is unique, how no two breaths are the same. Observe the texture, quality and duration of each breath. If you feel any tension, physical or mental, relax. Be patient and kind with yourself.
- Include any pain or physical discomfort in your field of awareness. Don't resist them. Use the breath to release the tension around the pain, imbue the breath with kindness. As you use

your breath to soften your resistance to pain or discomfort, you'll notice that the experience of pain is a constant flow of different sensations. Notice how they appear and disappear from moment to moment.

- Broaden your experience and notice the pleasant sensations. They can be very subtle, a slight tingling in the fingers; a well-being related to breathing; the sun coming through the window; the birds chirping outside. Observe your experience and notice the tiniest, pleasant sensations, however brief. Realise that every moment contains both painful and pleasant elements. That's what life is all about.
- Now realise that all of humanity experiences a mixture of pain and pleasure at every moment. Although we each have our own story, we go through similar emotions throughout our lives. We all have dreams and hopes, fears and anxieties, wherever we live, whatever our age, colour or social status. Feel how your experience of pain gives rise to empathy rather than loneliness.
- Direct kindness towards others. Feel the universal breath, like the movement of the oceans. Feel that you are part of this movement and dissolve the boundaries that separate you from it.
- Come back to full awareness of your body while lying in bed or sitting in a chair. Feel in contact with the earth. Tune in to the movements of the breath in your body. When you're ready, open your eyes and resume your activities. Try to carry this quality of presence with you in everything you do.

Visualising the Source of Power

- Sit in meditation posture, on the floor, on the bed or on a chair.
- Do some breathing exercises.
- Visualise in front of you a sphere of light, like a luminous drop, and consider that all the positive forces of the universe are gathered in it: love, compassion, regenerative power, etc. You can also visualise the Buddha or any other form or presence that makes sense to you.
- Feel its presence. Even if you can't see it very clearly, the most important thing is to feel it. If you're sitting in front of a fire, you'll feel its warmth whether you can see it or not. In the same way, even if it's imprecise, the sphere of light radiates an energy that can be felt.
- If the action you think is appropriate for your problem is one of appeasement, visualise a white sphere; if it is one of increase or intensification, visualise a yellow sphere; if it is one of control, visualise a red sphere; and if it is one of transformation, visualise a blue one.
- Give shape to your problem. If it's an illness, visualise the affected part of the body as a dark zone. The sphere of energy emanates rays of light that progressively dissipate and break up this dark mass. In the end, your body is completely luminous, without any blemishes or imperfections and radiating with positive energy.
- If it's a relationship problem, visualise in front of you the person or people with whom you are in dispute. Start by seeing them tense, perhaps even angry, but as they are touched by the light,

watch them relax and start to smile. If you feel any resistance to sending them good things, think that if they were happier, it would be easier to deal with them. Keep going until you feel that all tension is dispelled and that everyone wants the conflict to be resolved.
- Visualise other beings with the same problem as you and see how they are also touched by the rays of light coming from the sphere of energy. Feel happy when you see the transformation.
- At the end, imagine that the sphere dissolves into light and that the light dissolves into you and everyone you have imagined around you. Then spend a few moments relaxing in natural awareness.

Tonglen–Giving and Taking

- Sit in meditation posture, on the floor, on the bed or on a chair.
- Do some breathing exercises.
- Visualise a sphere of light, like a luminous drop, and consider that all the positive forces of the universe are gathered in it: love, compassion, regenerative power, etc. You can also visualise the Buddha or any other form or presence that makes sense to you.
- With each inhalation, feel the rays of light emanating from it dissolve into your heart. When you feel that your heart has opened, imagine the luminous sphere dissolving into it. Your heart is then transformed into a source of power identical to the one in front of you and endowed with the same transforming power.

- Imagine someone in front of you for whom you feel a great deal of affection. It may be someone you feel grateful for, like your mum or dad, or a defenceless being, like a child, an elderly person or an animal, who you feel inspired to protect. Imagine them suffering–in an actual or imagined situation–and let an immense desire to alleviate that suffering arise in you.
- Think of a specific situation in which you felt powerless in the face of someone's suffering. Let that wish take over.
- Then, without any hesitation, breath in the suffering of the person in the form of a thick black smoke. The smoke enters through your nostrils and goes straight to your heart where, through the power of the energy there, it is transformed into the light of happiness and well-being.
- Exhale. This beneficial light then comes out of your nostrils and dissolves into the beings in front of you, giving them immediate relief.
- Continue this exercise for as long as you wish, accompanying it with your breathing.
- Now imagine that another being comes join the first one–maybe someone who isn't as dear to you–and continue to take in their suffering and send them light and happiness.
- Keep adding more people, friends and foes, and continue to take in their suffering and send them light and happiness.
- In the end, imagine that everything dissolves into light and spend a few moments relaxing in natural awareness.

The three lights

- Sit in meditation posture, on the floor, on the bed or on a chair.
- Do some breathing exercises.
- Visualise in front of you a sphere of white light, similar to a crystal sphere, but transparent like a rainbow. This sphere has the power of all the positive physical energy of the universe.
- Visualise a ray of light emanating from the sphere and touching your forehead. Your body is filled with a sense of well-being. Feel that all negative actions are purified, all physical imbalances are harmonised and all illnesses are cured.
- If you suffer from an illness, concentrate on that part of your body. You can also visualise someone who is ill and direct the rays of white light towards them.
- Below the white sphere, visualise a red one. This sphere possesses the power of all the sound of the universe. Sound has an amazing power. Music influences our mental states and words can easily comfort or hurt.
- This vibrant red sphere emanates a ray of red light that touches your throat giving you a sensation of gentle warmth. All disturbances linked to sound and speech are pacified and you feel radiant with positive, warm energy.
- Below the red sphere, visualise a blue sphere, just like the previous ones, luminous and immaterial. Consider that it represents the spiritual energy of the universe. It emanates a ray of light that touches your heart and gives you a feeling of freedom and space.

- Feel that this light dissolves all petty, malevolent and negative mental attitudes, filling you with well-being, peace and goodness.
- Then watch the white sphere dissolve into a white whirlpool of energy that melts into your forehead. Feel that its transformative power is now part of you.
- In turn, the red sphere dissolves into a red whirlpool and merges into your throat. Feel that its power is now part of you.
- Finally, the blue sphere dissolves into a blue whirlpool and merges into your heart. Feel that its liberating power is now part of you.
- Dissolve the whole visualisation and rest for a few moments in a natural, relaxed state.

Practise so that these exercises become meaningful to you. Make them your own through daily practice until they become friends, refuges, a comforting presence in difficult times. You'll see that, day by day, you'll get a better sense of their deep meaning and positive effects.

TSERING PALDRON

ABOUT THE AUTHOR

Tsering Paldron was born in Lisbon, and moved to Brussels in 1973, where she first encountered Tibetan Buddhism. She completed a three-year retreat in the 1980s in France, under the guidance of Dudjom Rinpoche and Dilgo Khyentse Rinpoche, and with the supervision of Pema Wangyal Rinpoche. She received teachings from many lamas of all schools of Tibetan Buddhism.

She is a student of Ringu Tulku Rinpoche, and she has been teaching and travelling to teach at events or retreats since 1992. She also serves as translator for many Tibetan teachers, being fluent in French and English as well as her native Portuguese. You can find more about her by checking her website at www.tseringpaldron.com.

Printed by Amazon Italia Logistica S.r.l.
Torrazza Piemonte (TO), Italy